Entrepreneur Boot Camp® For Consultants

Essential Business Skills for Consultants.

Erik Bowman

Entrepreneur Boot Camp for Consultants
Learn more at http://www.EntrepreneurBootCamp.com

Copyright © 2012 by Erik Bowman, All rights reserved.

Written by Erik Bowman

Published by Guanzi Institute Press
legal@guanzipress.com
http://www.guanzipress.com
409 N Pacific Coast Highway, Suite 777, Redondo Beach, CA 90277

ISBN 0983786275
ISBN 978-0-9837862-7-6

Printed in the United States of America.

管
子
GUANZI
PRESS

Corporate, educational & volume pricing is available
on most titles. info@guanzipress.com
http://www.guanzipress.com

QR Codes Powered by Authr.com.
Get The App at http://authr.me/cKj

http://authr.me/cKg

Contents

Introduction

Be Your Own Drill Sergeant!

Unlike a typical military boot camp, in Entrepreneur Boot Camp® you have to be both your own drill sergeant as well as the recruit. You need to take control while at the same time be open to learning new skills, accepting advice & critique and learn how to start, run and grow your business. I have personally seen too many examples of aspiring entrepreneurs who open a new business without any forethought, planning or research.

"I found the perfect location for a tea shop so I signed a lease for the space."

Starting with a location and no plan is a condition that causes most businesses to fail. And it happens much too often. Location is secondary. You can have the best location but a poorly thought out business will fail. While having a second-rate location and well thought out business will succeed nine out of ten times. I know it's cliché but failing to plan really is planning to fail.

Planning your business does not end with your business plan, (if you've even written one). Planning is an ever evolving process. A great way to think of your business plan is as a "Living Document". Every day new opportunities will present themselves and you need to be prepared to accept them or reject them based upon where your business is at that precise moment and what your goals are. If a business doesn't move forward it will die, but before it does it will become stagnant and wither.

Re-Boot Camp

Lack of planning isn't exclusive to new businesses. Many people who have been in business for a few years and are "making a living" may not have a plan. Either through naivety, embarrassment or arrogance they stick to "what has worked in the past" and continue to eke out a living as their business flounders and ultimately folds.

Even seasoned business owners need the reality check of a Boot Camp; we'll call it a "Re-Boot Camp". A process whereby a seasoned business owner reassesses where their business is at and what opportunities they might find to increase their revenue and grow their business.

"Good thing you're not a Marine yet, because when a Marine quits HE'S DEAD!" –Anonymous

Boot-Up

Entrepreneurs need to learn to be self-motivating. I said "learn to be" because unlike the common misbelief, both self-motivation and entrepreneurship can be taught. I know this firsthand as I have taught hundreds of aspiring entrepreneurs through both the Certified Entrepreneur® program and Entrepreneur Boot Camp® events. There a three critical elements that you must practice to succeed.

Planning, repetition and execution are the core elements to becoming self-motivated. Self-motivation is the first step toward become an Entrepreneur. That's right, your amazing idea for a new or innovative business is not nearly as important as your self-motivation.

Beyond self-motivation are the business skills and knowledge you will need to startup and succeed. This book series is packed with both. You'll learn about business planning, legal issues, accounting, marketing, management and business growth. The skills, knowledge and wisdom gleaned from over two decades of personal Entrepreneurship, mentorship and teaching.

Why this book?

Entrepreneur Boot Camp® for Consultants is typically a live event with between 5 and 20 people interacting in a single room for nearly an entire day. It's extremely valuable to bounce ideas off like-minded individuals and receive guidance from a seasoned Entrepreneur who leads the event. Many aspiring Entrepreneurs (yes, even MBAs) do not have the core practical skills they need to even consider starting a business.

This book is designed with two purposes in mind; 1) As an educational pre-requisite for the live event; and 2) As a reference book to help the truly self-motivated Entrepreneur start a consulting business.

Educational Prerequisite

Attendees of the Entrepreneur Boot Camp for Consultants come into the event having tremendously varied backgrounds. They all have differing levels of academic education and work experience. We have found that nearly a third of the time has been devoted to leveling the playing field to make the conversations more impactful and meaningful. Using a book from the Entrepreneur Boot Camp series as a prerequisite to attending a live event creates a much more effective event and provides more time for everyone to fully see a benefit from the event.

Reference Book

Many people who aspire to start their own businesses do not have the ability, time or money to attend a live Entrepreneur Boot Camp event. I completely understand this. Simply reading this book will give you the foundational skills that will prevent you from making commons mistakes and save you thousands of dollars in typical startup costs. This book will help you make smarter decisions from day one.

Congratulations

So, whatever your reason was for picking up a copy of this book, be assured that you are making the first and smartest step towards business ownership. The skills and knowledge that you acquire from reading this book combined with your expertise and passion is the winning formula to make your business grow and prosper.

Here's To Your Success,
Erik Bowman

Welcome to Entrepreneur Boot Camp for Consultants

Consultants provide a great service to others, and therefore are held in high regard. By this point in time, you have probably determined that you possess unique skills and talents that set you apart from other business professionals, and that you would like to use these skills and talents to help others. That is the true essence of a consultant, and the reason why consultants are currently thriving in today's economy.

In this book, we will delve into the world of Consulting and show you all the steps you need to take to start your new business. With this book, you will learn:

- Who consultants are and what they do
- The many different types of consultants that exist
- What it means to serve others
- How to find your talent
- What it means to be an entrepreneur
- How to develop, finance, and start and grow a new business
- The reality of working as a consultant and how to determine your fees
- How to write a good proposal and contract
- Ways to find clients and how to market yourself
- The importance of networking and social media
- How to use project bidding websites to find work
- How to grow your business and why you should outsource
- How to be a manager
- Why you should join a consulting association
- Ways to give back to your community

By the end of this book, you will have a full understanding of the steps needed to begin, sustain and grow your new Consulting business.

The Business of Consulting

In this chapter, we will define consulting and outline what a consultant does. We will also briefly touch on the state of consulting in today's marketplace and the opportunities that lie ahead for consultants. By the end of this chapter, you will understand:

- What consulting is
- What consultants actually do
- What place consultants hold in the current market and the opportunities available for the future
- How to find your unique talent and determining who your clients are

Who are Consultants and What Do They Do?

Think of Consulting as a very large umbrella that can cover all manner of services. Any definition we can give you isn't terribly specific. And that's because as a consultant, you will be providing a specialized service to fit a need, and that can be just about anything that requires expertise. But, we'll start by giving a general definition.

Consultant
A person who possesses a certain talent, skill or expertise that when applied can improve the situation of another individual or business.

Now, let's take that definition and add a little more specificity to it. Consulting really begins with talent. Without a specific talent or expertise, you have nothing to offer anyone else. A successful consultant is one who possesses a skill or expertise that others are willing to pay money for. The more specialized and highly regarded the skill and expertise, the more money people will be willing to pay. The people whom consultants serve are generally called *clients*. Although you can also use the terms *buyer*, *employer*, *customer* and even *consumer*, we will stick to the term *client*.

What a consultant really does is use their skills and expertise to solve problems for other people. So saying that a consultant is a trained problem solver is probably more accurate. Not only should you be able to help people with their particular problem, you must *want* to help people in the first place. As a consultant, helping people will be your number one priority. If that doesn't interest you, then at least you've not read past the beginning of this book. If you know you want to use your talent to help others, then keep reading.

But first, who are consultants? Well they can be anyone, really. Most people might think of consultants as management consultants – those people who come in and help steer large businesses in a more profitable direction. However, there are many consultants outside of the corporate arena.

And the list goes on. Just about any service that someone could want can be provided by a consultant. The bottom line is this: when you are selling your talent and expertise to another, you are acting as a consultant. Consultants are essentially entrepreneurs, as they are their own boss and have essentially created a new business by which they sell themselves.

But what do consultants actually do? The answer can be just as varied as the many different types of consultants, and really depends on the job. A consultant usually is called in to either provide advice for a business or single employer based on their knowledge and expertise in a field. However, some consultants provide a physical service outside of just advice. For instance, a freelance writer is using their writing skills to write a document, report or advertising campaign for an employer. The freelance writer, or consultant, is not a long-term employee, but usually only a short-term hire for a specific project. When the project is done, the writer will invoice the employer and get paid for their services.

> **Here is a partial list of types of consultants**
> financial advisors, accountants, financial planners, copywriters, creative writers, web designers, graphic designers, marketers, public relations, landscapers, gardeners, architects, computer programmers, software designers, administrative support, client service representatives, cosmetics salespeople, stylists, personal organizers, home stagers, interior designers, nutritionists.

Usually what marks a consultant is that they are in fact their own business, not the employee of another. A consultant is a temporary hire, usually by written contract, and is only hired to cover a specific task, problem or project. When the work is done, the consultant is paid and the contract for service is considered complete. Now, it's not always this simple. As you can see from the previous list, there are many different kinds of consultants over many different fields and industries offering different skills and talents.

What traits make for a good consultant? This question is a little more difficult to answer as there are so many types of consultants. However, there are a few basic personality traits that will help an individual in pursuing this kind of work.

Helpful Personality Traits for Consultants:

- **Confidence in your abilities**. People are placing their trust in a consultant, and no one will trust a consultant who does not appear sure of their abilities.
- **Flexibility**. Consultants serve others, which can also mean serving others' needs before your own. It helps if you are

flexible enough to work around your clients' needs first and foremost.

- **An articulate speaker**. Part of being a consultant is communicating your abilities and suggesting solutions to clients. Being able to be easily understood is integral to success.
- **A good listener**. Consultants must first and foremost understand how they can help their clients, and this involves listening closely to what is needed and expected by the client.
- **The ability to easily communicate abstract ideas**. A consultant needs to be able to present concepts and ideas to a client in a way that is easily understandable. Before being hired, a consultant must always present a proposal outlining what it is they can offer the client. Your proposal needs to clearly communicate what you can do and how.
- **A sense of humor**. Consulting at times can be very frustrating, especially when dealing with demanding clients. By maintaining a sense of humor and not letting your work dictate your moods, you'll be able to handle any situation.
- **Patience**. Finally, a consultant needs to have patience. Consulting is a business about relationships, and relationships take time to develop. You need to have enough patience to see your projects and relationships through to a successful outcome.

So now that we have discussed who consultants are and what they do, let's talk a little bit about the history of consulting as well as the myriad opportunities available in today's market for new consultants.

Present and Future Opportunities

Consulting has been around for centuries, though we didn't always call it by the same name. History is filled with individuals who provided services to other individuals for a price. All monarchies had consultants, though they were called advisors. As long as there has been industry, there have been those with knowledge who assisted others with that knowledge. So by becoming a consultant, you are actually taking on a profession that has been around for centuries. Consulting as an identifiable industry is really more of a recent phenomenon. The rise of large consulting firms, hired by even larger corporations, in the last 20 years has helped foster a view of consulting as a big money profession. However, the truth is that the money made by consultants is really quite varied.

While the traditional view of a consultant is one who charges a hefty hourly fee - a fee that only big businesses seem able to pay - these days you can find consultants in all price ranges. The lowering of prices is most likely due to the large boom of available consultants across all industries and all nations. This larger pool of consultants has created more competitive pricing so that smaller businesses and individuals are now able to consider using a consultant whereas before they wouldn't have the budget to do so. What this means for you, the consultant, is that you need to determine what value your services have and what price your market is willing to bear. We'll talk about setting your price later in chapter 3.

As for the future, consulting opportunities seem to be cropping up everywhere, every single day. There has never been such a high demand for consultants as there is now. Perhaps it is because businesses see that they can actually save time and money by hiring an expert for a project who is remote, versus hiring a full-time employee and having to pay overhead costs for their space in the office, as well as a salary, benefits and money towards a retirement plan. Also, thanks to the explosion of the internet, businesses and individuals can now hire consultants from anywhere in the world. Consultants can be hired when they are needed, often on short notice, and then when the job is done, the employment is over.

The benefits of using consultants:

- Provides an outside perspective that is completely objective
- Lower office overhead
- Reduce or avoid paying salaries and benefits
- Hire only when you have a need
- Project-based versus full-time employment
- Costs vary depending on level of expertise
- Can find an expert from anywhere in the world
- They work independently and need little supervision
- A temporary consultant is cheaper than a full-time employee

Since businesses have begun to see the benefits of turning to consultants, the consulting business is experiencing a boom. So if you've always dreamed of starting your own business and working from home, now is the time to do it. But first you must consider what it actually means to go into business for yourself. Next we will look at the pros and cons of working as a consultant.

Pros and Cons of Working as a Consultant

Consulting might not be for everyone. While there are consulting firms for which many consultants are merely employees, most consultants are in business for themselves or if they are a part of a business, it is usually a very small one. In this book, the assumption will be that you are entering into consulting not to be hired by a large consulting firm, but instead to start your own firm or be an independent consultant. Either way, there is a certain amount of business know-how you will need to possess to be your own boss.

The following are some of the pros and cons of consulting.

PROS OF CONSULTING	CONS OF CONSULTING
Flexible hours – you set your own schedule	Finding work is not guaranteed and can be inconsistent
Can work from home	Need to be more responsible with your time and accountable to yourself
You can set your own rate	Less social interaction than an office atmosphere
Income potential is unlimited	No guarantee you'll get paid on time, or at all
You keep 100% of your profits and can utilize many tax write-offs	You will owe self-employment and business taxes in addition to income taxes
There is no limit to the number of projects or clients you can service	May require long hours to meet deadlines followed by periods of inactivity
You control the amount of taxes you pay the IRS quarterly.	You must pay quarterly or annual tax on earnings based upon an IRS form 1099

Working for yourself requires a lot of self-discipline and responsibility. However, it also brings great freedom and flexibility. Not everyone is suited for life as a consultant. It will require you to be an honest judge of your value and your time as far as setting your rates. However, since you have something to offer, there is no limit to what you can charge if your service is in need. If the work sounds appealing to you so far, then let's move on to talking about determining what talent you have to offer.

What Is <u>YOUR</u> Talent and <u>WHO</u> Do You Serve?

Everyone has a talent to offer, it is just a matter of determining what that talent is. For those who have worked for many years in the business sector, you may have accumulated a breadth of knowledge in a certain field. For example, a long-time loan officer for a bank might find they possess a financial know-how that is of value. For others, you may find you have a creative talent that is of use for businesses or even individuals, such as a photographer with a good eye for capturing human emotions. Before you can take a single step towards working as a consultant, you will need to figure out what you have to offer and how you can turn that into a business.

Finding Your Talent

What comes first: the talent you have or the type of consulting you want to do? Both are very important. For you to put in all the hard work to start your own business, you must love what you do. However, it will be easier to be successful if you have a true talent for what you want to do. Everyone has a skill or expertise that is of value. The trick is determining what that is. Below are just a few questions you should ask yourself when looking to find what it is that you are truly good at and also what you are not good at. Knowing what *not* to do is critical in determining what you *should* do.

Questions to ask yourself when looking to become a consultant:

- What is my passion?
- If I could be anything what would I be?
- What do I know that might help others?
- What experience do I have and how much of that experience can I pass on to others?
- If money were no object, what would I do with my time?
- Do I like to work with people, or do I work best alone?
- Am I creative? If so, how?
- What am I really good at?

- What have other people said I am good at?
- What am I not good at?
- What have other people said are my weaknesses? My strengths?

For some of you, if you've spent many years working in one type of industry, that is a clue to what knowledge and expertise you will want to capitalize on. For others, maybe it's a passion you've had as a hobby, such as creative writing or photography, which you now want to devote your time to. Whatever it may be, you cannot move forward until you have settled on exactly what it is you want to sell, because that is really what you are doing as a consultant – selling yourself.

Next, you need to take your talent and think of how that talent can be turned into a business. Let's say, for example, you have a talent for numbers and you have experience preparing budgets very accurately and easily. Great. Perhaps being a financial consultant is your calling. But that is still very broad. You now need to determine how to use that talent to help others. Will you be a financial planner who helps individuals and families get their finances in order and save money for the future? Will you want to help small businesses by preparing financial plans and operating budgets? Will you sell yourself as a personal accountant who can help individuals and businesses with their taxes? The possibilities are endless. And some answers may require you to get more training, while other answers may show you are ready to start today. Start thinking about *how* you can use your strengths and what kind of business you will need to create to sell those strengths.

The last part of determining your talent, is determining if there is a market for that talent. When you want to consult, you need to know if there is a demand for the expertise you want to offer. You will need to start doing some research about your desired industry. Look up others who are doing the same thing, check out the competition. Browse help wanted ads and see what services people are actively looking for. If you can determine there is a need for your desired service then you are one step ahead of the game. Below are some questions to ask when looking to research your market.

Questions to answer when researching potential clients:

- Who are your potential clients? Are they individuals? Young or old? Businesses? Big or small?
- What do your potential clients *need*? What do they *want*?
- What are your potential clients currently spending on this type of service, if they are using it at all?
- What can you offer your potential clients that is different from other competitors?

The main reason for going into business for yourself is making money, so first determine if there is an opportunity to do so. Next, we will talk about what specific service you will be providing your potential clients.

Serving Others

The first function of a consultant is to service others. What good is a skill if there is no one to benefit from it? After you have decided what your talent is, and what industry you belong to, you need to clearly state how you can help others. It's almost like writing your own personal mission statement. Once you know your service, you will know how to sell yourself and where to focus your advertising. Below are just a few examples of types of consultants, and the specific service they provide.

Consultant Type	Service
Financial Planner	Help young people and new families save and invest their money for future retirement
Videographer	Provide others with a DVD of lasting memories for their biggest life events like weddings, birthdays and anniversaries
Web Designer	Help individuals and small businesses create a visually stunning and easily navigable web site to promote their businesses

Once you have determined you are ready to serve the needs of others, you then need to sell your services directly to them. A big part of being a consultant is being a salesperson. You need to let your target clients know that you have the skills and know-how to help them. When you genuinely want to service their needs, they will know and the "selling" part won't be so hard. If you can always remind yourself that you are here to serve above all else, then you'll find that selling your services comes fairly easily. Below are some basic steps that all consultants follow when helping others.

Steps to Consulting:

1. Determining the need to be filled / problem to be solved.
2. Researching and preparing pertinent information.
3. Complete any necessary tasks to fill the need / solve the problem.
4. Present the final result.

Even though consulting comes in many forms, the steps to complete or deliver services are pretty much the same whether you are solving a problem for a business or completing a specialized project that they need to have done. Before you begin, the next question you will have to ask yourself is how many hours you are willing to devote to your new business.

To Quit Your Day Job or Not – That is the Question

For some people, starting a new business and working as a consultant is something they want to begin while currently employed so as not to go without any income. While the benefits of being self-employed includes the ability to work when you want to, trying to only work nights and weekends won't get you very far when you have clients who need you during the week. Therefore, it will be difficult over time to hold down a full-time job and also start a new business. There is a lot of hard work that goes into starting a new business, and it will require your complete focus. However, if you are passionate about your new career, all the hard work will be worth it.

There are plenty of people that decide to hold down a regular job and consult on the side. For some professions, especially the creative ones like writing and design, it can be easy to consult part-time on off hours. But for others, especially anything business or financial related, you will need to be available during regular business hours.

But the real test is how secure you are in beginning a new business while being currently unemployed. If you are unsure of going into business for yourself, then it may be a good idea to give consulting a try in your spare time. However, if your dream of being a consultant also includes owning your own business, then you need to treat consulting as your new full-time job. In the end, whether or not to pursue consulting full-time is your decision.

In Conclusion

Hopefully, by the end of this chapter, you have decided that consulting is your true calling. You have determined your unique skills and talents that set you apart, and you have researched the market to verify there is a need for your service. You have also defined what it is that you will do, and how you will service others. Finally, you are ready to dedicate your time to starting your new consulting business.

In the next chapter, we will discuss entrepreneurship and give you the steps you need to take to start a new business.

How-To Start Your Business

In this chapter, we will give a general overview of what it means to be an entrepreneur and own your own business. We will give you a basic guide to starting your new business, as well as how you can go about finding the necessary financing to begin. We will also talk about intellectual property and how to protect your rights. By the end of this chapter, you will understand:

- The concept of Entrepreneurship
- The steps you need to take to start a new business
- What Intellectual Property is and how to protect it
- Ways to finance your new venture

An Overview of Entrepreneurship

Before you can start working as a consultant, you need to fully understand what it means to *be* in business for yourself. When you become a consultant, in essence you will be starting a business. This means you are now a business owner and entrepreneur as well as a consultant.

As a business owner and entrepreneur, you will be responsible for every facet of your consulting business. This means that you need to understand the basics of *starting* and *running* a business. We will take a moment now to provide a brief summary of what you need to know and do in order to operate your business. If this is your first foray into entrepreneurship,

---

Entrepreneur

An individual, who germinates the idea for a new product or service, takes responsibility for the new idea, implements the necessary steps to bring that new idea to the marketplace, and thus creates a new enterprise.

---

then it is strongly suggested that you take the **Certified Entrepreneur Program** offered through Guanzi Institute. This in-depth program will take you through every stage of starting a new business, and leave you with a full understanding of what it takes to be a successful entrepreneur.

But even if this is not your first business venture, it never hurts to refresh on the basics of entrepreneurship. So let's get started.

Entrepreneurship

When you become an entrepreneur, you are undertaking the responsibility of starting a new business and managing the entire process from start to finish. It begins with a new idea for a product, or in this case a service, developing that service, researching the target market for your service, and then formulating a business to deliver that service to potential clients. Entrepreneurs must have drive, patience, and be willing to do the hard work necessary to turn that new idea into a successful new business. The good news is you are your own boss. The bad news is you are your own boss. If you don't possess the know-how of how to start and run a business, then the chances of you succeeding are not high. That is why you are reading this book and hopefully taking the Certified Entrepreneur program.

Entrepreneurs continually challenge the market by taking initiative, finding new and creative ways to service the consumer, and revolutionizing the way business is done. Most startups are in fact small businesses. But don't let those words scare you. According to the Small Business Administration, **small businesses account for 99.7% of all employer firms, and employ just over half of all U.S. workers.** Some believe that small businesses are the future of business. And the statistics seem to support that belief.

Small businesses currently dominate the marketplace and their constant development and evolution year after year helps bring new jobs to the workforce. So rest easy knowing that you have picked a great time to go into business for yourself. However, don't be fooled into thinking that the path itself is easy. There will be many steps that you need to take in order to begin your new business. Next, we will cover how to plan and finance your new business.

Planning and Financing a Start-Up

Creating a new business can be a lengthy and tedious process, but if done right, it will be extremely rewarding. Below are the many points we will cover in this section:

1. Choosing your business entity
2. Strategy, Planning, and Research
3. Budgeting
4. Writing a Business Plan
5. Finding Financing

When starting a business from scratch, on the other hand, there is still a lot of ground to cover, so first up is deciding what type of business you are going to be and then creating the appropriate legal entity.

Business Entities

Before you can begin doing business, you will need to officially set up your business entity. There are several different forms of legal business structures, all with their own pros and cons. We will review them briefly.

The first big step in deciding which legal entity to choose is determining what service you are offering others and how you will deliver that service. If you are selling a single service, then a sole proprietorship may be your best bet. If you require a financial investment from someone other than yourself to begin, you may want to look into a Limited Partnership or LLC. If you plan on hiring employees and eventually expanding your business, you may want to consider a larger structure such as a Corporation. Only you can make this determination. It is advisable that you seek out legal advice from a qualified professional when looking to start a legal business entity, as the rules and requirements differ by State. We will briefly highlight the structures below before moving on to the planning and research required to begin a business.

- **Sole Proprietorship**: Owned and operated solely by only one person who is entitled to 100% of the profits, but is also responsible for 100% of the business and its expenses. The sole proprietorship has no separate identity outside of the owner and the owner pays personal income tax on all earnings. Most sole proprietors do business in their own name or use a fictitious business name (DBA) which we will talk about later in this section.

- **General Partnership**: Consists of two or more individuals who come together by contributing money, time, expertise and resources to begin and operate a business. Unless stated differently, the partners have equal share and pay personal income tax on any earnings. To begin a general partnership, the partners will draft a written partnership agreement.

- **Limited Partnership**: A partnership where one or more partners are general partners with personal liability and the responsibility to manage the business. The other partners are *limited* partners, meaning they contribute capital and share in profits but have no say in the management of the business and their personal liability is limited to the amount of their investment into the business. There must be at least one general partner and at least one limited partner. To create a Limited Partnership you must file a Certificate of Limited Partnership with your state.

- **Corporation (C-Corp & Sub-Chapter S)**: These are the only entities that pay their own taxes, with members paying personal income tax on any profit they receive from the business. A corporation is a completely separate entity from the individual owners and investors (referred to as shareholders). Shareholders must transfer capital into the business in exchange for shares or stock and their liability is limited to their investment. Corporations must be overseen by a board of directors that serves the interests of the shareholders. They must file certain reports with the state and also follow definite formalities or they can risk losing their corporate charter granting their existence.

  - A **Sub-Chapter S Corp** is allowed to have all profits and losses pass through to the shareholders instead of taxes being paid at the corporate level, thus losing the aspect of double taxation. An S-Corp though has limitations as far as number and types of shareholders as well as types of stock that can be issued.
  - A **C-Corp** has no restrictions on number of shareholders or types of stock and has elected not to pass through profits and losses. Therefore, taxes are paid at the corporate level and then the

shareholders pay taxes on their income received from the business.

- **LLC**: An LLC is neither a partnership nor a full-fledged corporation, although it blends aspects from both. It is a separate legal entity, but is not required to sell stock. An LLC is taxed like a partnership (no entity taxes) but the members have the limited liability protection of a corporation. There is no limit to the number of members, and other corporations or partnerships can be a member.

A Word on DBAs (AKA Fictitious Name Statement)

If you are starting out as a self-employed consultant, then a Sole Proprietorship may be the best choice to start. Sole Proprietorships will require that you apply for a DBA so that at a minimum you can **D**oing **B**usiness **A**s (DBA) a name other than your personal name. The other legally organized business entities such as a Corporation, Subchapter-S and LLC are already entities unto themselves and as such do not require a DBA.

You will want to have a DBA so that you can establish a separate business entity outside of yourself, especially when it comes to your finances. With a DBA you can open a separate business checking account that will allow you to keep your business and your personal finances separate. That way, when a client issues your business a check, you can deposit it directly into your business bank account. You will not be able to cash a check made to a business name unless you have the official proof that the business exists, thus the DBA.

DBAs are easy to obtain and the application fee is very small. However, the entire process can take 4 to 6 weeks to process and you will not be able to set up a business banking account until the process is complete and you have an official DBA certificate. If you are going into business as a Sole Proprietorship, then obtaining your DBA should be your first cause of action before you begin doing business, or else you will have to do business under your personal name in the interim.

Research, Planning and Strategy

Before you can take the physical steps to starting your business, you need to spend some time researching, planning and developing your strategy. A *strategy* is a plan of action created to achieve a goal. When looking to start a business, you need to determine what your goal is and how you will reach that goal. Your business strategy will cover the following points.

Business Strategy Questions to Answer

- What you will sell – what is your product/service?
- How much money do you need to produce your product/service?
- What is your market and who are your consumers?
- How long can you operate before you need to make a profit?
- What is your overall goal? Is it to make a profit? Grow into a bigger business? Or sell your business for a profit?
- How will you reach that goal?

The answers to the above questions will begin to form your business strategy. You need to know what you are selling, how and to whom, and how much money you need to begin. It may seem easy, but finding the answers to these questions can take some time. Don't rush this part of the process, as a poor strategy will spell doom for any fledgling business. Once you have the answers, you need to formalize your business strategy by putting it in writing.

Business Strategy Outline:

1. Your vision for the business.
2. Your end destination.
3. Goals to reach that destination.
4. Define your market.
5. Define how your business will operate.
6. List the resources you need to get started and to operate on a day-to-day basis.

What will require the most work is your market research. It can be tedious but it is imperative that you determine if a market exists for your product or service and that you know the ways to reach that market. We will talk about that research next.

Perform Extensive Market Research

Before you even think of beginning your business, you must assess if there is a current demand for the product or service you want to provide. Just because you want to sell something, does not mean you have the

---

TIP: When performing market research; be sure to closely study your competitors. By truly understanding what your competitors offer to their consumers, you can then find ways to offer something better. You can also study who their market is and what ways they advertise and promote to that market. Anything you can learn from your competition will be a great help in devising your business strategy.

---

opportunity to do so. Opportunity in the market is present when a demand exists for which there is no existing product or service to <u>fully</u> satisfy that demand. Without demand by the consumers, there is no profitability for a business.

You do not have to create a new product or service that doesn't already exist. However, you must make sure that the product or service you want to provide has more demand than your competitors are able to fill. You need to have a market.

Before you set up your business, think ahead about how you would market and promote your product or service to your future consumer. Therefore, you must research the market. There are many websites where you can obtain current market information. Try www.business.com or www.marketresearch.com for current listings. Even www.wikipedia.com is a great resource for market research.

To determine the viability of your product or service, you will need to determine the following:

- Current state of the economy in regards to consumer spending.
- Pricing structure for similar products or services.
- Current consumer demand and predictions for future quarters.

Budgeting

When starting a new business, you will need to know how much money it will cost you to start your business and how much money it will take to operate your business day-to-day. You need to develop solid numbers before you can begin looking for money, because when pitching your business plan to potential investors, you are making assumptions about how much money you need from them to get started and how much money you (and they) can expect to make in the future. Therefore, these assumptions need to be based on solid numbers.

There are two types of budgets you need to run; a startup budget and an operating budget. These budgets will be included in your business plan that you will be using to secure financing for your new business, so make sure that you are honest in your projections.

- **Startup budget:** The cost to begin a new business including the fees and costs associated with renting an office, setting up utilities, opening a bank account, creating a website, purchasing or leasing equipment and supplies, and printing marketing and promotion materials.
- **Operating budget:** The monthly and annual costs of keeping your business running, including overhead costs (such as rent, utilities, and salaries), any dues and fees, and ongoing marketing and promotions.

It is a good idea to have a clear picture of how much up-front money you need to get started as well as how much money it will take for you to operate for a full year after you begin doing business. Most new business owners make the mistake of only budgeting for starting the business, not running the business. It can take months, or worse years, for a business to break even or begin realizing a profit. Therefore, you need to know if you have enough money available to not only start your business, but to keep it running for up to a year in case you do not start making money right away. There are several financial planning mistakes you need to avoid when creating your budgets. We will list some dos and don'ts below.

Financial Planning Dos and Don'ts

- Don't underestimate your startup costs.
- Do plan some room for error (a *little* overestimation is okay).
- Don't underestimate the time it will take to bring in revenue.
- Do plan on having enough money to cover your operations without any revenue for one year (to be safe).
- Don't overestimate your income potential.
- Do study your competition and use their sales as an example.
- Don't expect financing to happen overnight.
- Do be prepared to begin without financing.

The last point may be difficult to accept, but it is not wise to *completely* rely on others to fund your business. We will talk more about financing later on.

Write a Business Plan

Lastly, before starting a business you need to have a sound business plan in place for not only how you will operate day-to-day, but also how to go about funding your new business. Unless you have a stockpile of money saved, you will most likely be looking to other people for money. To do this, you will need to present them with a well-researched business plan.

This will be the most important document you will ever write for your business. Not only will it become a blueprint for how to run your business, it will allow you to begin looking for investors to fund your business. Typically, entrepreneurs must rely on family, friends and acquaintances to get the money they need to start. However, if you have a well-written business plan you will be able to approach potential investors when seeking money.

LEARN MORE

http://authr.me/cJS

We have provided a sample business plan for you at the end of this chapter.

You can also visit http://www.entrepreneurbootcam p.com for an electronic version perfect for editing. Or scan the QR Code to download immediately.

Financing

Before you can jump into doing business right away, you will need to solve the problem of financing your business. If you have tons of money saved away, then this step may not be an issue for you. But still, you might not be comfortable with using up all of your hard-earned money for your business. Seeking financing is not only a common practice; it can be a smart way to start a business.

Most beginning entrepreneurs usually look to friends and family for capital, as they are not only likely candidates, but you already have a relationship with them. However, not everyone has friends or family with money and not everyone is comfortable asking those they love to donate or loan money that might never be repaid. New businesses are risky and there is a chance any investor can lose their investment. However, if you have done all of your planning and research and have determined that a strong need exists in the market, hopefully you will be prepared to succeed.

So for the purposes of this book, we will assume you are looking to find financing *outside* of yourself and your friends and family. First off, we will talk about equity financing.

Equity Financing

When looking to acquire financing for your business, you may want to look to bring in individual investors; those people with enough money to invest into your business. However, no one

> **Equity Financing**
> The offering of ownership in a business in return for

will ever just give you money with nothing in return. People expect to be repaid, either the amount of their investment plus interest or with a percentage of profits. When you look to finance by offering equity, you will be doing the latter.

When offering equity, you are in essence asking an investor to give you money in return for a portion of ownership in your business. This is different than incurring debt, such as taking out a bank loan. When you have debt,

> **Capital**
> The net worth of a business; that is, the amount by which its assets exceed its liabilities.

you are obligated to pay that debt back along with a pre-determined rate of interest. With equity, an investor is not being paid back by you. Instead, they

have a stake of ownership in your business and can receive profits. Or, they can lose money. That's the risky nature of business.

Finding an equity investor means you need to find someone who is willing to take a risk for either making money or losing money up to the amount of their initial investment. However, you will have to determine how much ownership of your company you are willing to give away in exchange for capital to begin.

Depending on how your business is organized, you will have to work out with your investor their stake of ownership. If you are a corporation, you will be issuing stock to these investors, which is just another form of ownership. If you're not a corporation, you will need to be able to offer investors some form of liability protection so they can only lose up to the amount of their initial investment. You can do this by forming either a Limited Partnership or LLC.

One last word about equity financing – as a first time entrepreneur who only has a good idea, and no track record, you may find yourself faced with investors who will offer you small amounts of money for large portions of the business. You have to decide if you are willing to give away the control of your business (meaning you have less than 50% ownership). If this does not sound like an appealing proposition, you can either revisit your friends and family or look towards debt financing.

Debt Financing

If you are unable or unwilling to give up a portion of ownership in your business to an investor, then you may want to look towards debt financing.

There are many pros and cons to borrowing money. In the end, you need to take into account your financial situation and weigh that against the terms you are being offered.

> **Debt Financing**
> When a business borrows money for operations or new purchases can be either long-term or short-term.

Advantages of Debt Financing	Disadvantages of Debt Financing
Money can be acquired quickly	The money must be paid back
The costs are apparent so you can easily budget	Your debt repayments will decrease your monthly cash flow
You retain 100% ownership of your business	May be required to personally secure the debt therefore, you are personally liable and your personal assets are at risk

Debt financing may be the easier way to go, but you are paying for it. Also, debt will increase your liabilities and the repayments will decrease your cash flow. But, you are retaining all of your profits since you have not taken on a new owner, so the disadvantages may be worth it to you. Below we will discuss the many different forms of debt financing.

Forms of Debt Financing:

1. **Bank Loans**. Bank loans are the most common form of debt financing. A bank will usually require your business plan as well as other forms of financial documentation. Interest rates can be high, but you will know your monthly obligation beforehand and you'll be better able to budget. You will, however, have to personally guarantee the loan.

2. **Small Business Administration** (www.sba.gov). The SBA has a number of loan offerings for small businesses, especially those that are struggling in finding a bank loan. The SBA will guarantee the loan. Since the loan still goes through a traditional bank, your loan terms and repayment plan will be no different than if you obtained a bank loan. There is usually a limit on the amount you can loan through them, but they can help you get your business off the ground.

3. **Credit Cards**. Credit cards are, unfortunately, a popular way many small businesses finance their fledgling ventures. While it may seem easy at the offset, most credit cards companies charge high interest rates that can accumulate very quickly. You will need to treat a credit card investment just like any loan, and repay the amount as quickly as possible.

4. **Home Equity Line of Credit**. A Home Equity Line or HELOC is when you borrow against an asset, usually a house. You are essentially placing a lien on your property in the form of a second mortgage that will be paid back as if you are paying back a loan.

5. **Retirement Funds**. Another way to access cash is by using funds in a self-maintained retirement account like a Roth-IRA. Withdrawing money from these accounts is not without consequences, so make sure you fully understand the penalties and taxes associated with using this money before you consider it.

6. **Life Insurance Policy**. You can also borrow against your life insurance policy if it is a whole life policy. This will be treated as a loan that you will pay back over time. If you should die before the loan is repaid, then the payment from the policy will be lessened by the outstanding balance.

7. **Private Debt**. *Private debt* is obtaining a financial contribution from an individual that you will treat as a personal loan and pay back with interest. Instead of offering equity, you are offering a promissory note that that can either be secured (backed by an asset) or unsecured. This form of debt can be risky for the investor, so they may require a much higher interest rate in return for taking on the risk.

8. **Combining Equity and Debt Financing**. What most entrepreneurs find is that by combining equity and debt financing, they have a much more manageable situation. This way, you can give away only a portion of your ownership and then obligate yourself to loan repayments for the remaining capital you need. By offering investors a promissory note that they can have the option to convert to equity in the company, you can harness the best of both worlds.

Friends, Family, Angel Investors and Venture Capital

As we stated earlier, sometimes utilizing friends and family for cash is the quickest and easiest route. However, there are "angel" investors as well as venture capitalist funds that might be good resources for raising capital. The following list will outline each of them.

1. **Friends and Family:** When borrowing money from those you know, be sure to offer them a promissory note in return. It's a way to legitimize your transaction, and shows that you respect them enough to want to pay them back.

2. **Angels:** *Angel investors* are individuals with an extremely high net worth who choose to invest in young, fledgling companies. They're called angels because they are a blessing, but extremely difficult to find.

Check with your local community and state to see if there are any Angel organizations where you can possibly meet and network with these individuals.

3. **Venture Capital:** *Venture capitalists* are individuals who invest their personal money in new startup businesses. A *venture capital fund* is usually run by a company or individual that oversees the money placed in the fund from many sources. They then look to invest fund money into new businesses. This is different from angels in that it's usually market and industry specific. Also, to obtain venture capital money you will need to go through a thorough review and when given money you'll abide by a strict set of provisions. Venture capitalists can offer the most amount of money to a new business, therefore the rigors of obtaining it are well worth it.

Before anyone makes a determination of whether or not to invest in your company, they will be performing a valuation of your business plan to see if the business appears sound.

Tips on How to Present your Business Plan to an Investor

Yes, you need a solid business plan in order to entice an investor. No one wants to invest in a losing proposition. They only want to invest if they believe that they will make. However, *how* you present your plan is just as important as the content. Sometimes by personally taking investors through your plan, you have the ability to show your knowledge of your business, convince them you are fully prepared, and get them excited about your product or service. Below are some tips on putting your best foot forward when looking to secure financing.

Tips for pitching your business plan:

- Know your plan backwards and forwards and be prepared to answer any and all questions relating to the material you have provided.
- Use audio/visual aids to get your point across. Even if you have a PowerPoint presentation you may want to prepare slides for an overhead projector or blow up photographs and statistical graphs as a backup. People are influenced by visuals.
- Rehearse your presentation. Pick keywords and phrases you want to emphasize, then practice your "speech" and rehearse using all of your visual aids.

In the end, people will be investing in you as well as your business. Show them how excited you are about your new product or service and they will be excited in return. Now let's move on to talking about the steps you need to take to physically start your business.

Starting a Startup

Once you have decided on your business entity, researched your market, written a sound business plan and have secured financing, you can begin taking the necessary steps to start your new business. Below, we will walk through the startup process. For an easy to use checklist, see Appendix 1: Basic Business Startup Checklist.

1. **Name Your Business!** When you start a business, you will need to think about creating a brand. *Branding* is crafting an image for your product and your company that will be instantly recognizable and your image begins with your name. A good business name will be one that is identifiable to the business you are providing. A strong link between your name and your product or service will help attract consumers before they learn anything else about you. When you create your legal entity you will first need to search the Secretary of State Business database in your state to

make sure that the name you want is available, and then register the name. Once you have your business name, you can use it on all of your marketing materials as well as when you are designing your company logo. **Be sure to check that your intended name and logo is not currently trademarked by another company. We will talk more about trademarks and other protected property under the legal section of this chapter.**

2. **Prepare a startup and operating budget.** Before you can begin doing business, you need to determine how much money you will need to get started as well as how much money it will take to operate your business for the next 12 months. Therefore, your first official task will be to devise your budgets, then obtain the necessary funding if you do not already possess it. Below are the many things you will need to consider when setting your budget.

   a. **Overhead Costs.** Overhead costs include your rent or mortgage and utilities. This also encompasses the services required to keep your business running such as phone, internet and website hosting fees, email server and any salaries and benefits you will be paying. When doing a startup budget, you need to list the cost of getting these services set up. Some rental contracts require 1 or more months payment in advance, and utility companies usually have an installation fee, so you need to know the overall figure for each and every service you will be using. After you have set-up your services, you will need to budget the ongoing expense of these items.

   b. **Insurance.** Yes, you will absolutely need insurance so you might as well budget for it. Insurance will cover you and your business in the event of an unforeseen disaster, loss or lawsuit. Some common kinds of business insurance include General Liability, Property (whether you own or rent), and Business Interruption (due to business closure because of damage). At the very least you will need liability insurance. It is best to consult with an

Insurance Agent or Broker to determine what insurance you should carry.

c. **Licenses and Permits.** Some businesses require a permit or license to operate. You will need to check with your state and city to see what the requirements are for your industry and budget for the expense. Check the License and Permit tool at http://www.entrepreneurbootcamp.com for specific legal requirements in your area.

d. **Legal costs.** There will be some legal costs for certain business entities. It is best to consult with an attorney to see what is required for your desired legal structure and then budget for the fees necessary to obtain the required documentation as well as obtaining any trademarks and patents, if warranted.

e. **Marketing materials.** Before you can perform your service and make money, you will need to find potential clients. Spending money on marketing materials is an absolute necessity at the very start. You need to budget for the expense of advertising as well as marketing through other outlets such as social networking. We will talk about marketing more in depth in chapter 4.

f. **Equipment and supplies.** Finally, you will need to determine what equipment you need to purchase, lease or rent and any supplies you will need. Items you need to finance are: computers, printers, scanners, phones, answering systems, postage machines, paper supplies, general office supplies, and any specific items you need to provide your service. Again, budget the initial expense for purchasing, or the monthly cost of leasing these items, as well as a monthly expense for maintaining these items.

g. **Taxes.** You will have to pay taxes on your income; there is no way to skirt around the IRS. Therefore, it is in your best interest to budget ahead of time for the estimated amount of taxes you may owe at tax time every year. Most financial professionals will tell you to set aside 30% of your income to pay your taxes. You will need to determine what is smartest for you. But don't make the mistake of setting aside *nothing* for your taxes or you will find yourself in a financial pinch when your taxes are due. Businesses not only pay the federal government, they pay state and sometimes city taxes. Therefore, it is wise to budget between 20-30% of your expected income for taxes.

3. **Set-up your home base.** What you first need to determine is <u>where</u> you will be doing business. The reason we say *home base* and not *office* is because these days, more and more entrepreneurs are choosing to work from home offices. A home office is a great way to save money when starting a business, though it does not work for everyone. Whether you will work out of your home, or you will be renting office space, you need to have systems in place to communicate with clients, perform your tasks, and then receive payments.

   a. **Home vs. Office.** There are pros and cons to working from your home. When you work from home you save on overhead costs as well as commute time. However, you will not have a formal office in which to meet clients face-to-face. Renting an office will take a larger initial investment and will cost you more in terms of utilities and furnishings, but you will also have an official place of business. Which direction you go really depends on the most important needs of your business and how much money you have to start. If you are working on a limited budget, working from your home is the smartest solution. Then when business picks up, you can consider relocating to an actual office.

   b. **Outfit your work space.** Next, you will need to have all the equipment needed to operate a business such as a desktop computer with internet access, a laptop computer for traveling, dedicated landline phone, personal cell phone, printer, scanner, as well as abundant office supplies (i.e. pens, pads, paper). Even if you currently have a computer, you need to have a top of the line computer with plenty of free hard drive space. *You are in business now, and you need to have the best equipment possible to work in the most efficient manner.* Think of your office equipment as an investment. You will get to claim these purchases as a deduction on your taxes, so don't skimp! Work the price of new equipment into your startup budget. If purchasing equipment is still outside of your budget, then consider leasing instead. Leasing business equipment is a great way to avoid using personal credit and it will allow you to stretch payments out over 2 to 5 years. Visit http://www.entrepreneurbootcamp.com for more information about outfitting your new business through leasing or scan the QR Code to open immediately.

LEARN MORE

http://authr.me/cJT

4. **Determine how you will operate.** When talking about *operating* a business, what we mean is all of the tasks required to run a business day-to-day. This includes office administration, sales and billing. When you work for yourself, you will be doing everything. You will need to determine how you will get paid and when as well as how you will deliver your product or service.

5. **Apply for any required licenses and permits.** Some businesses are required to have a permit or license to operate (i.e. Contractors, Plumbers, etc.). Some cities require all businesses to obtain a business license and/or permit if you plan on doing business within city borders. You will need to check with your state and city to see what the requirements are, if any, for you to operate your type of business. You should check with your Secretary of State as well as your City Office of Finance. Some permits and licenses can take weeks or

months to acquire, so be sure to check ahead of time to avoid any delay in beginning your operations.

6. **Get Online!** These days almost all businesses have a presence online and those who don't are missing out. When starting your business, you will need to set up a website which includes a way for clients learn about your company, discover what products or services you offer and to contact you by phone or email. Most new entrepreneurs today are creating web-based businesses that operate solely online. It is an easy way to sell goods and services to clients from all over the country and even the globe. Engaging in business over the internet constitutes *E-Commerce*. More and more clients use the Internet has their main channel for locating new products and services. Your top priority needs to be creating a website for your business and determining how you will offer your services to your clients. Below are the basic steps in creating a website.

> **LEARN MORE**
>
>
>
> http://authr.me/cJU

a. Choose your domain name (AKA website address) and register it.
b. Find someone to host your website.
c. Build and design your website.

There are companies that can do all of the above at a low monthly or annual cost. They will not only register your name for you, they will host your website and offer you many easy to use website templates so you can essentially create your site yourself. Check out sites such as www.verisign.com, www.GoDaddy.com, www.iUtility.com.

7. **Hire an accountant, bookkeeper or buy accounting software.** When going into business for yourself, you will have to keep track of your finances. This can be difficult for those business owners who do not have a background in finance. Hiring an accountant is a wise decision. If you cannot afford to hire an accountant long-term, then at least hire one temporarily to help you set up your books. Both Quicken and Peachtree are great accounting software programs that are easy to use for owners with limited accounting knowledge. However, you will need to refresh on some accounting basics so you know the difference between an asset and a liability. Below are some steps you need to follow before your business can begin handling financial transactions.
   a. Set up a business checking account.
   b. Take inventory.
   c. Hire accountant/purchase accounting software.
   d. Set up your books with your assets and liabilities.
   e. Enter financial transactions weekly.

8. **Devise your marketing plan and obtain the materials.** Now that you have set up your business, you need to find customers. A business only makes money when it succeeds at selling something to someone. You cannot trust that customers will simply find you, you will need to market your business. To service people, you need to know what they want, find ways to provide for that want, and then let them know that you exist to fulfill that want. We will discuss marketing in more depth in chapter 4.

The above steps are very broad and if you need more detail about any of the above topics, you can check out the **Certified Entrepreneur Program**. Now, let's talk about some legal issues that you need to be aware of.

Intellectual Property

Before moving on to working as a consultant, we need to discuss a few legalities, namely intellectual property. *Intellectual Property* is an intangible asset. Patents, trademarks, copyrights, and trade secrets all fall under intellectual property. When starting a business, any creative thought or invention can be protected by law. You can protect the product/service itself, the product/service name, your methods and processes, your packaging, and/or your overall design.

What is important to understand about intellectual property is that not only do you have a way to protect your brand, you will also have to be very careful to make sure you are not infringing on another business' protected rights. However, once you have a claim to your own intellectual property, you are protected from violations by others.

Below we will briefly talk about the different types of intellectual property, and the steps you need to take to protect yourself.

Types of Intellectual Property

- **Patents**. A *patent* gives the exclusive right to hold, sell and license a specific product or service, even a specific method. If your idea is new and innovative and if you've already physically developed this idea then you can file for a patent, though what constitutes a patent is a very gray area. To apply, you will fill out an application and provide a full and detailed explanation of your invention (product, service or method). You have 1 year after you have publicly introduced or sold your creation to apply. Visit http://www.uspto.gov for an application.

LEARN MORE

http://authr.me/cJV

- **Trademarks**. A *trademark* is legal protection for a word or symbol or both. However, they must be used in such a way that either the word or symbol completely identifies the product/service and/or business. Despite the business name, you can also trademark a shape, animal or even a color; if again, it completely identifies your business. There is no legal requirement to file for a trademark for a trademark to exist. However, it is advised that you file nonetheless. You should perform a proper search to make sure any trademark you consider using is not already in use by another company to avoid any legal entanglements. Whether you file with your local patent and trademark office (in the U.S. go to http://www.uspto.gov) or simply wish to claim a trademark, you should immediately place the letters "TM" after your company, product or service name and logo.

- **Copyrights**. A *copyright* protects anything that is written. The problem with copyrights is that the scope is very broad. Copyrights can include books, catalogues, lists, manuals, advertisements, photographs, websites, film, video & audio works, architectural designs, computer software and hardware. The copyright only covers what is actually written, not the overall idea. You cannot copyright an idea, only the form and manner in which the idea is presented. Just by creating and publishing something, a copyright is formed; you do not need any formal identification. But just like trademarks, it is suggested that you register your material anyways. To register, you must first contact the U.S. Copyright Office at http://www.copyright.gov for an application.

- **Trade Secrets**. A *trade secret* is any personal knowledge that you possess that needs to be kept a secret so that you have a competitive advantage above other businesses. This can range from secret methods, formulas, techniques, promotion strategies down to consumer lists, where you get your materials, and the nature of your supply deals. To protect what you consider a trade secret, you must draft a Non-Disclosure Agreement and have everyone who knows the secret sign it. Finally, it is up to you to take the proper steps to make sure all of your internal documents are marked "confidential."

When you are creating a new business, you will inevitably have processes, identifiers, and other secrets you want to protect. By not protecting your property, you risk your hard work being stolen and capitalized on by others. However, if you know the law and take the proper steps to protect your rights, you will be prepared for any infringements that may occur.

In Conclusion

In this chapter, we have discussed starting a new business. We covered entrepreneurship and what it means to be your own boss. We talked about planning and financing your new venture, as well as listed all the steps you need to take to begin. Lastly we covered some legal points, namely intellectual property.

Now, without further ado, let's move on to the next chapter and talk about what you need to know before you start working as a consultant.

Working as a Consultant

In this chapter, we will discuss how a consultant operates day-to-day. We will talk about determining the fee you will charge for your services, questions to ask clients when trying to sell your services, and what a proposal is and how to write a good one. We will also cover consulting contracts, as well as managing your progress. By the end of this chapter, you will understand:

- How a consultant works
- How to determine what to charge for your time
- Questions to ask potential clients at your first meeting
- How to write a winning proposal
- Writing an employment contract
- How to be your own project manager

First Step ... Talk to Other Consultants

Now that you are prepared to do business, let us take a moment to discuss the realities of working as a consultant, as well as how to establish your fees and formulate contracts. A good idea to begin with is to talk to other people who are already working as consultants. You can learn the most from people who are currently consulting than you can from any book. Seek out consultants in the industry you would like to enter and ask them about what they do. It's a great way to learn, and it's also a valuable networking tool that may help you down the line.

When talking to other consultants you will want to first and foremost determine how they work, what terms they work under and also what rates they charge. It will be helpful to see what works for them and what doesn't. And don't talk to just one consultant; seek out as many as you can! After you have talked to a wide range of working consultants, you'll begin to see what sets some apart from others, and you can begin to decide how you would like to work. With that said, let us turn to how to determine your fees that you will charge your clients.

How-To Set Your Fee

Deciding how much to get paid as a consultant is not as easy as it may seem. You need to be competitive but also place an honest value on your time and abilities. There's also the question of how much your potential clients will be willing to pay for your services. If you set your rates lower than your competitors, you may be flooded with clients and not have enough time to complete your tasks. Or even worse, you may be working too many hours for not enough money. Set your rates too high and you may watch your potential clients balk and choose to work with someone else. Finding the right balance will take time.

Below are some things you need to keep in mind when considering what to charge for your services:

- You need to earn enough money to cover your expenses
- To gain clients you will initially need to charge in the ballpark of what other consultants in your field are charging.
- You need to decide if you will charge an hourly rate or a flat fee per project.

The good news is, as you are essentially a temporary hire for a specific need, you can experiment with your rates as you work more and more. However, you will need to start with a basic rate that you will advertise in order to find your first clients. Before we start talking about how to determine this rate, let's discuss the difference between an hourly rate and a flat fee.

Hourly Rate versus Flat Fee

You will find many different opinions among consultants about the proper way to charge for your services. Traditionally, consultants are hired based on an hourly rate. Whether it's $25, $100 or even $500 per hour,

> **TIP:** A good rule of thumb in determining your rate is to charge double what you need to make to survive. For example, if you can break even by averaging $25 per hour, then you should charge double that amount. As a business owner, you now have to pay more in taxes as well as business insurance and even personal health insurance and other benefits.

consultants have traditionally kept their time worked on a project and then billed the client for the total number of hours worked. However, there has been a rise in consultants who charge a flat fee for their services on a project by project basis. This pricing method places a value on the services the consultant is offering versus the time spent. While many consultants choose to stick to an hourly rate, there are more and more businesses that are looking to hire consultants for a project fee versus an hourly rate.

Only you can determine how you want to do business, though you may find that some fields lean towards one method. Many writers, graphic designers and programmers are beginning to work for flat fees. While other types of consultants, mainly financial and management consultants continue to mostly charge hourly.

Here is another point to consider. You may find that by moving from time-based billing to project-based billing, the potential for income is much higher. This is because there are only so many hours in a day, thus only so many hours you can work in a week. By placing a value on your service, and charging based on that value, you may find your income potential is much higher when using a flat fee versus an hourly rate.

What most consultants do to determine a flat fee is estimate the amount of time it will take to complete a given project, assign an hourly rate and then multiply that by the total number of hours. The drawback is that you may end up working more or less hours depending on the project. Although, after you've worked enough you'll be a pretty good judge of how long it will take for you to complete a project.

That leaves us with – how do you decide what to charge? The smart answer is – charge somewhere in the middle of what those in your industry are charging.

Try setting an hourly rate that is somewhere in the middle of what others are charging. You don't want to be the highest price, but you also don't want to be the lowest. If you are at the lowest rate, you will get clients, but because the rates are so low, you will end up working a lot of hours for little money. If you are offering flat fees for services, for example a flat fee for designing a website, then again choose a fee that is somewhere in the middle of what others are charging. Once more, you will need to make sure that you will make enough money to cover your expenses as well as make a profit.

Price versus Value

One last thing to keep in mind when determining your fees is that you are creating a *value* for your services and not setting a *price*. When your bid is based solely on price, then your clients will make a decision on whether or not to hire you based on your price. But when you place a value on what you can offer and communicate that value to your potential clients, then you will be hired based on the value that you can bring to your clients, not your price.

As we discussed in chapter 1, part of finding your talent is determining the unique skills that you can offer that will set you apart from your competition. You will be gaining clients based on those unique skills. If you can convince your clients that your unique skills are of a benefit to them, they may not look at your price as the determining factor in whether or not to hire you. The more perceived value you have, the more you can charge. And that's a main reason why you have gone into business, to make money.

Selling Yourself at Your First Meeting

Part of being a consultant is selling you and your services. This may be disconcerting for some people, but in fact it is a requirement of the job. To gain clients, you are essentially pitching to them what you can offer. This is usually in the form of a written proposal (which we will talk about a little later) but can also be during a face-to-face meeting.

When meeting with potential clients you have a chance to examine their situation and then determine exactly how it is you can help them. People are coming to you with a problem to solve or a project to complete to gain a desired result. They want to know that you not only fully understand what it is they need; but that you can offer them something different than anyone else they will be talking to, as most clients usually shop around.

The best way to really sell your service is to ask a series of questions during your initial meeting so that you not only fully understand what it is they need, but you can determine exactly how you will assist them. Below are some general areas you need to cover in your initial interview, and some example questions you should ask.

Questions to Ask Potential Clients when Selling Your Services

1. **Determine if you are appropriate for the project**. First, you need to see if you are even a match for what the client desires. This will save you from wasting your time, and the client's time, if you cannot assist them. Try to determine what it is they desire and what parameters they want to work under.

   Question: What is it you hope to accomplish?
   Question: What is your budget for this task?
   Question: What is your time frame for results?
   Question: What skills are you looking for?
   Question: Are you committed to this project or are you analyzing whether or not you wish to proceed?

2. **Determine who is responsible for the budget.** When working with an individual, there is no need to determine who is footing the bill. However, things can get tricky when you are dealing with a medium to large scale business. You need to determine who is responsible for funding the proposed project so you know if the person you are talking to has any power over paying you.

   Question: Who has the power to approve this project?
   Question: Who controls the budget?
   Question: Who is in charge of the results?

3. **Determine the objectives for the project**. Before you can decide if the project is worth your time, you need to have the client clearly state exactly what parameters they expect and what duties they wish to be performed as well as their desired result so there is no surprise down the line.
   Question: Why are you seeking to do this project at this time?

Question: *What specific tasks do you want accomplished?*

Question: *What exactly do you expect to have at the conclusion of this project?*

Question: *How will this project help you?*

4. **Try to assess the value**. When talking to a potential client, you need to always try to ascertain how important this project is to them. Determining the value they place on the project will help you in setting your price. When a project is of an enormous value, then a client is willing to pay to obtain the best value possible. However, if the project is of little value and is more speculative, then you may realize that they will not be willing to meet your fee and you can move on.

Question: *How important is this project to you and/or your business?*

Question: *What is the impact you are hoping this project has?*

Question: *How important is this project to you in relation to your other duties?*

Question: *If this project is not a success, how will that affect you and/or your business?*

5. **Look for more opportunity**. Anytime you meet with a potential client, you have a solid business lead. Don't limit yourself to the project you are meeting about. Ask questions to see if there are other opportunities for related projects for the individual or even for other areas of the business. You won't know until you ask, and every opportunity counts.

Question: *Can I provide you with a variety of options versus just one?*

Question: *Are there other areas in your business you are looking to improve?*

Question: *Are there others in your organization looking to do the same?*

Question: Would you like me to assist you in measuring the results?

6. **Attempt to close the deal.** Never leave a meeting without an offer of employment if you can help it. A big part of selling is closing the deal. If you don't push for a sale, you can bet another consultant will. Always try to leave with a promise for more.

Question: If you are happy with my proposal then when can I start?
Question: How soon can I be expected to begin?
Question: Is there anything else you need to know before making a decision?
Question: How soon after I give you my proposal can we speak again?
Question: Are we good to go?

Whenever you get an opportunity to speak to a potential client about your services you need to ask questions. If you don't ask, you won't get any answers. The more you do it, the better at it you will become.

Writing a Proposal that will Close the Sale

First, part of being a consultant is creating a proposal that outlines what you can offer your clients. Then, when you are hired by a client you will need to make a contract that states what you are being hired to do, how much you will be paid or what your hourly rate is and an estimated time of completion. First, we will talk about writing project proposals.

Before you get hired on as a consultant, you will most likely be asked to submit a proposal. Not all fields require this, but a proposal can come in many

DOWNLOAD

http://authr.me/cKb

forms. A proposal really is a summation of what services you are going to provide, how much money these services will cost, what value they will bring to the client, and how long the service is for. It's almost like a sales pitch, just a more formally written one.

A good proposal is one that will highlight the value you are bringing to the client as well as the project objectives, deliverables and a suggested timeline. You will clearly outline the rate or fee, as well as list any milestones or check-in points along the way where the client can review what has been done so far and ask any questions and offer feedback. A proposal can also be called a *bid* when done online through the many freelance project bidding websites that are available. We will discuss these in detail in chapter 4.

Usually submitting a proposal to a potential client comes after you have had an initial contact and created a relationship, and then the potential client invites you to send in an offer of how you can help them. Therefore, the proposal really is your selling point and can either make or break your chances of gaining the business. **Proposals need to be clear, concise and convincing.** If done right, they will close the sale for you. If done wrong, you may lose the sale or need to have further meetings in order to convince the client to hire you.

The following are the major points you will need to include in your consulting proposals as well as some dos and don'ts.

Consulting Proposal Points to Include with Dos and Don'ts:

- **Your qualifications and experience (why select you?).** You always need to give a brief synopsis of your background and specific talents. But there's no need to go into too much detail. **DO** remind the client of why you are a great choice and why you have the skills they need. **DON'T** make this section too long or work too hard to convince the client that you are qualified. They have already chosen you for a proposal, so trust that they already feel you are qualified.

- **Overview of proposed project.** This is your chance to go over the project that you have previously discussed with the client. **DO** make sure to include all the points that they want covered as it will demonstrate that you fully understand what the client wants. **DON'T** include points that are outside the scope of what was discussed, otherwise the client will feel that you are attempting to expand the project for your own benefit.

- **Expected outcome.** Clearly state the objectives that the project will to accomplish. You want to show that you understand the expected outcome and what benefit the project will bring to the client. **DO** list all of the objectives as well as the overall value that the project will bring to the client. **DON'T** be vague with what is expected, as a vague proposal can lead to the client asking more from you than you are prepared to give.

- **Expected deliverable.** The deliverable is different than the outcome. An outcome is the benefit that the project will bring; a deliverable is the physical form of the project that you will be presenting to the client upon completion. **DO** clearly outline what it is you will be preparing for the client. **DON'T** make the mistake of promising a deliverable that you cannot deliver.

- **Steps you will take to achieve the outcome**. You need to outline for the potential client what steps you will be taking to achieve their expected outcome. This is also your chance to present options, so the client can be involved in the process. By listing options the client will begin thinking of how they want to use you instead of whether or not they want to use you. **DO** list options of how you can perform the expected task, all reaching the same result. **DON'T** be vague about your methods or the client may choose someone else who has provided them with specific details.

- **Price: flat fee or hourly rate (if hourly list estimated number of hours).** One of the main things a client will be looking for is how much you will be charging. **DO** be very specific in what you are charging the client. No one wants to feel that they are being taken advantage of. If you are hourly, you need to give a clear estimate of your expected hours. **DON'T** ever give a price range, as it is human nature to want and expect the lower price, and a client may be upset if the price is on the upper end of the range. If you give a firm price in your proposal, then there are no surprises when you present your invoice.

- **Payment terms and conditions**. The terms and conditions portion of your proposal will cover everything from how you will be paid, when you will be paid, what expenses you will bill the client for (if any), and any other fees you will be charging. **DO** give exact methods for payment and timelines. **DON'T** be unclear. If you do not state how and when you want to be paid, a client can easily take advantage of the situation and stretch out payments for their benefit.

> **NOTE:** Payment terms are critical for consultants. Most clients will prefer to pay the entire fee when the project is complete. However, that may not cover your costs as you work and can lead to problems down the road if the client is late on paying or decides not to pay at all. Always try to ask for a certain percentage of the fee upfront, and/or set-up a schedule where a portion of the fee is paid after certain steps or tasks are achieved and approved. That way you have cash flow while you work.

- **Timeline.** You will need to state for the client how long you expect the project to take, as well as when you can begin. Timelines are very important for clients as some are working on a tight turnaround. There is nothing worse than taking longer than you proposed. **DO** be honest about your time, and give yourself some leeway. **DON'T** promise a time frame that you cannot adhere to. If the client knows ahead of time the expected timeline, and agrees to it, then you have nothing to worry about. If you were off on your projection, you can run the risk of having an un-satisfied client.

- **Signature page**. Even though most proposals are just that, proposals, you should always include a place for the client to sign off indicating that they accept the proposal. You will still need to draft a contract if the proposal is accepted, but having an acceptance page will help you easily close the deal.

Usually a proposal happens after there has been an initial meeting, or talk, between the potential client and the consultant. The proposal then is really just a summation of what the client has communicated that they require and what the consultant has communicated they can provide. It is not a legal contract; that comes later once the client has accepted the proposal and decided they want to hire the consultant.

After submitting a proposal, it is suggested that you follow up with the potential client after a reasonable amount of time (a few days) to see if they have any questions or concerns. Try to have a conversation either in person or over the phone versus email. Once you have the job, it is time to prepare a contract.

Creating a Contract that Protects You

Once a proposal is accepted, the consultant must draft a contract for the agreed upon service.

A contract can be oral or written, though it is highly recommended that you get into the habit of always providing a written contract. A contract will vary depending on the client and the service that they require, although you will be able to work off of a template for most of your contracts and then adjust it to fit the specific terms of each project. At the end of this chapter, we have a sample

DOWNLOAD

http://authr.me/cKc

consulting contract for you to use as a guide in creating your own. For the most part, all of your contracts will have the same components.

Consulting Contract Points to Include:

- The terms from your accepted proposal: project scope, deliverables, expected outcome, and timeline for milestones and overall completion.
- The acceptance by both parties of the proposal terms.
- The consideration for the proposal – meaning the agreed upon value (the fee) and the terms of consideration (payment terms).
- Be very firm in your details of what you will do to avoid scope creep. *Scope Creep* is a project management term for when an employer keeps adding additional project requests and even increases the scope of a project without warning. A project that is not clearly defined can run the risk of being infinitely re-defined by the employer, thus creating more work for the consultant than they initially planned. To avoid scope creep, make sure you have clearly outlined the project, and have a clause about what an employer must do when they wish to alter the terms of the project.

TIP: Be sure to have your legal advisor review all contracts before you sign them. Having a 'boiler plate' contract for your services is advisable since you only have to pay your legal advisor once (assuming your client is agreeable to all terms.

Contracts can be as simple or as complex as you make them to be. Although making a lengthy contract filled with legal jargon may sound like good protection for you, it's actually bad business for independent consultants in the long run. You are offering a personalized service, and people want to deal with a person not a legal department. Cover your bases in the shortest and simplest terms possible. In the end, you are officially setting forth the terms of the project, as well as the agreed upon timeline and fee from your proposal. Once it is signed by both parties, you have a working contract. It doesn't need to be hundreds of pages long or take you weeks to prepare. A simple document of only a few pages is all you need.

Being Your Own Project Manager

When consulting you are not only the worker, you are also your own manager. When taking on a project as a freelancer, you are responsible for managing that project and making sure all of the agreed upon steps are taken. Regardless of how you are billing your client, hourly or flat fee, you will need to keep track of your time so that you know how much time you are spending on each phase of the project and can estimate your expenses. For consultants, it is suggested that you create a daily activity log of your time. You will need to document the date, the time spent and total time for each activity. You can keep time in any increment you prefer. Below is an example of an activity log with time kept in 15 minute intervals.

Daily Activity Log

Date	Time Start	Time End	Activity	Total Time
1/22/10	9:00 a.m.	10:30 a.m.	Review financials received from Client A	1.50 hours
1/22/10	11:15 a.m.	11:30 a.m.	Email Client A regarding financials	0.25 hours
1/23/10	7:00 a.m.	1:00 p.m.	Create Operating budget for Client A	6.00 hours
			Total Time for Client A	**7.75 hours**

Again, if you are billing a client hourly, a daily time log is an absolute must. However, even if you are working for flat rates, it is smart to keep track of your time so that you can gauge how much time each project takes you, which can affect what you charge for similar projects in the future.

As you work on your projects, you will also need to keep track of any expenses you incur, such as office supplies, gas and mileage for traveling, etc. It is a way to not only keep your own business budget, but you can potentially use these expenses as write-offs for your taxes.

Once your project is complete, it will be your responsibility to invoice your clients. Invoicing should always be done promptly according to the payment terms you set in your contract. Check out the appendices at the end of this chapter for a sample invoice for an hourly rate, as well as a sample invoice using a flat fee for services.

Should You Bill for Reimbursable Expenses?

Another factor you will need to consider when consulting is whether or not to bill your clients directly for your reimbursable expenses. A *reimbursable expense* is a business expense that you incur directly due to a project or task, such as any postage, supplies, phone calls, and travel expenses. Whether or not you bill the client directly for these expenses is up to you. However, it must be clearly stated in your proposal and contract that you are passing along these expenses and the client must agree beforehand.

Some clients will expect that your rate will include any expenses you may incur, so be sure to communicate this issue beforehand with all of your potential clients. If you are charging a flat rate for services, you can estimate any business expenses and include that as a part of your flat fee.

Collecting on Late and Delinquent Accounts

Every consultant, from time to time, may encounter a client who is either late on paying their bill or simply refuses to pay. It's an ugly side of business, but it does happen for any number of reasons, and not always related to the satisfaction of your services. How far you choose to pursue past due and unpaid balances is up to you. If you fight too much, it can end up incurring you more expenses in the long run and you still might not be paid. Legal action is expensive, and sometimes your clients may have more money than you to pay for legal defense if legal action is taken.

If you have set up partial payments in your contract or if you make it a practice to always request a retainer upfront, then unpaid balances will be less of a worry. A *retainer* is an upfront fee paid to a professional either before services begin or on a monthly basis to be available for services. If a client misses a payment, you can simply stop work. However, if you have waited to be paid until the completion of the project, then pursuing further action will most likely be a benefit to you. Below is a list of steps you can take when looking to collect on late and past due balances.

Steps to Collecting Late & Unpaid Balances

1. **Contact the client directly**. Always try to reach the client and engage in a conversation, either by phone or email. It is courtesy to attempt to communicate, as there may be any number of reasons why they are late.
2. **Send a second invoice**. Another method is to re-send your invoice with a notice on there that it is past-due. No need for any threatening language. Just a reminder that there is a balance and the time to pay has passed.
3. **Send a letter from an attorney**. Have a local attorney write a simple warning letter asking for what you're owed and possibly offer a 10% - 20% discount if the client pays promptly, as a lawsuit will not be good business for either party. The letter has a good chance of working and shouldn't cost more than a couple of hundred dollars.
4. **Call a collection agency**. If all other communication methods have failed and it has been a reasonable amount of time in which the client hasn't paid (at least 30 days), then you can look to a collection agency. A collection agency will pursue the balance due and take a percentage. This can be pricey, anywhere from 20% and up, and there is no guarantee that they will ever get a payment from the client.

5. **Take legal action**. This is a very expensive step to take, and also can drag on for months. When attempting legal action, always try mediation or arbitration first, where a third party can help settle the dispute. If no agreement can be reached, you'll have to go to court (and pay lawyer fees to as well).

Having clients who do not pay can be angering and frustrating. However, you need to weigh the consequences of taking legal action against the loss you will incur if you simply never get paid. Sometimes it may be better to just get on with your life, and protect yourself better in your future contracts by either requesting a percentage of your fee be paid up front or implementing partial payments during the length of the project.

In Conclusion

In this chapter, we have given you the tools to work with as a consultant. We discussed how to determine your fees, how to write project proposals and employment contracts, as well as how to be your own project manager.

In the next chapter, we will discuss ways for you to find new clients, market your services, network with other professionals, and why you need to get online and use social media as well as the many project bidding websites that aid consultants in finding work.

Finding, Reaching & Selling to Clients

In this chapter, we will discuss the best ways for you to go about finding clients, notifying them about your new business and selling your services. This will include mainstream marketing channels, as well as online social media and other web-based project bidding websites. By the end of this chapter, you will understand:

- How to create a successful marketing strategy
- Ways to look for potential clients
- How to use the internet and social networking to your advantage
- How to use online project bidding websites and place a bid
- Marketing and promotion tips you should employ

Marketing Yourself

Serving people is really what all businesses do. Determining the needs of the client and then finding ways to advertise and promote your service to that client falls within a business marketing strategy. *Marketing* is the strategy to find clients and then promote your product or service to entice clients to buy your product or service. *Advertising* is a specific action taken to promote a product or service and *Promotion* is the overall act of communicating with the public to influence them to buy your product or service.

Now that we have the definitions down, let's talk about the steps you need to take to create a marketing strategy for your new business.

1. **Research your client.** Before you can market to potential clients, you need to know who your potential clients are. When researching the market, look for who is most likely to buy your product or service, then look at their spending habits and what they value when looking to purchase that particular product or service (i.e. quality, best price, etc.). Once you know who you are selling to, you will know how best to reach them.

2. **Check out your competition**. It is also best to take a look at what your competition is doing. By studying your competition, you can determine what methods they are using to advertise and promote their products or services, and it will clue you in to some good methods for your own strategy. This is business after all and you need to take advantage of every successful idea and conversely, you can see what isn't working and then find a new direction.

3. **Develop a brand**. Before you begin printing up your materials, you need to develop a clear identity for your business, also called branding. Below are some branding tips.
   a. **Pick a name that stands out**. Your business name should clue clients in to what you do or at least

stand out. This name will be used on all of your official papers and materials so choose wisely.

b. **Design a logo**. A *logo* is either a graphic design or image that gives a visual to your business and business name. For example, if you offer a home cleaning service, your logo might be a mop and bucket. Your logo will identify you as much as, if not more than, your name and will be used on all of your business materials.

c. **Create a catchy slogan**. A *slogan* is a saying that captures what you are selling in one sentence. It will describe what it is you are selling in a creative and memorable way. The slogan will also be used in your promotional materials next to your business name and logo.

d. **Have stylized text & imaging**. Lastly, you will need to decide on the font and color of your business name, logo and slogan. This same text and color choice will be on everything your business does, from company letterhead, to invoices, to packaging and all advertising materials. If done consistently, clients will begin to recognize your business, and recognition is the key to branding.

4. **Create a promotion strategy**. Now that you have designed your business' image, you need to determine the ways in which you will promote your business directly to clients. There are many different channels through which to advertise. You may not be able to afford to do them all, at least not all at once. A good promotion strategy will only focus on a few areas at a time so that you can be consistent. Below are some of the many methods you have to choose from.

a. **Television, Radio and Print Advertisements** (local, state or national). Using TV, radio, newspapers and magazines are a great way to quickly spread the word over a large area, however they are the most expensive option and there are plenty of other methods that are just as effective. If you have the money, try sticking to popular seasons and holidays for national coverage.

b. **Direct Mail campaign**. With the rise of email, direct mail campaigns are not as effective as they used to be. However, they can be worth it when used in conjunction with other methods, such as an email campaign.

c. **Email campaign**. An email campaign is sending newsletters, flyers and ads directly to a client's email inbox and it is a great way to keep current clients updated on upcoming sales and promotions. You should avoid sending emails to those who are not currently your clients (i.e. SPAM). Also, a good email can travel far by becoming *viral,* meaning the recipient may forward the email to one or more of their contacts, who may also forward it on, and so forth.

d. **Web Banners** (on other websites). A web banner is when you place an advertisement for your business on popular websites for a fee. When your banner is clicked, users will be routed to your website. Pricing for this method varies and depends on the host website. Try to target websites in similar industries (i.e. placing your photography services on a wedding website).

e. **Craigslist or other free community websites**. Craigslist is a mostly free community website for most major cities in the U.S. Here you can post the services you are offering while you get your marketing campaign off the ground. It's good to have a presence in your local community even if you're global, and keeping a presence on Craigslist is always a good idea. Also check and see if your community has any other websites or community publications you can utilize.

f. **Social Networking sites**. You need to have a Facebook, Twitter and LinkedIn account solely for your business. That way, you can offer discounts, answer questions and generate viral marketing for your business. Each service offers fan pages, groups or lists where you can further promote your company's products and/or services. We will talk about these sites in more depth later on in the chapter.

g. **Cross-marketing with other products and services**. Sometimes teaming up with a related but non-competitive business can be most cost-effective. For example, if you are a photographer maybe team up with a make-up artist and/or stylist for a promotion.

h. **Outdoor signs**. The use of billboards, banners and outdoor signs in any commercial area in top geographic markets can help promote your business.

i. **Seminars, workshops and trade shows**. Holding a seminar or workshop, free or for a price, to highlight your product or service is a great way to develop interest among potential clients in many local communities. By giving people a taste of what you can offer, you are more likely to have them decide to continue to use your products or services in the future. Industry specific trade shows are another great way to reach a group of people, and all it takes is a booth and your product or service on display to market your business.

j. **Word of mouth**. The oldest and probably most reliable method. Spreading word of your business through your contacts is very effective, especially if you are also taking other steps to increase your network of contacts. We will talk about networking next.

k. **Online Affiliate program**. An *online affiliate program* allows third-parties and even existing consumers of your product or service to act as independent sales people. There are many service companies that can manage an affiliate program on your behalf or you can purchase and install software to run one yourself.

l. **Start writing articles, blogs or even a book**. There are a large number of social bookmarking services, article hosting sites and even blog sites where you can start writing about your business, your industry or the economy in general. Sharing your thoughts and insights on business can help increase the visibility of you and your brand. To go even further, you may want to write a book if you feel that you have gained enough skill and expertise to pass on to others. A book can be used as a very impressive business card. When you meet someone new, be it a client or a business associate; imagine handing them a signed copy of your book!

5. **Work on retaining current clients**. After you have found a client, you want them to keep buying your product and service. With all of this talk about finding new clients, part of a good marketing strategy is also finding ways to *keep* your clients. You should always be thinking of different promotions, sales and discounts to offer your current clients to keep them wanting to use your product or service. By retaining current clients, a business can help ensure steady revenue over time.

6. **Ask for referrals.** Referrals are a great way to build business, especially if you are recommended by current satisfied clients or other business professionals in your community. Since you are being personally recommended, a lot of your work is being done for you. It might be smart to implement a promotion or discount for clients who refer others to you, so they have an incentive to bring you business.

7. **Develop quality control systems and ways to handle feedback**. You cannot please everyone all of the time. At one point or another you will have to deal with a dissatisfied client. The good news is dissatisfied clients are valuable if you can obtain feedback from them about what went wrong. When a client is unhappy with your service, it is best to always hear them out (let them complain) and then offer a solution. Then follow up after a short period of time to see how the solution worked. All businesses will lose some customers, it is inevitable. But if you have a way to deal with unhappy ones, you will lose less over time. The truth may be hard to hear, but complaints will always lead to you

improving your product or service and you will make more money in the long run.

8. **Create a timeline and budget**. All marketing strategies need to have a clear timeline of goals and a budget. As a new business, you will most likely not have enough money in your budget to run advertisements every day. You need to set up a timeline. Decide when you will promote and when you will not, focusing on different promotions for different seasons. When making a timeline, always have an end point in sight. After a certain period of time, you need to step back and see if your marketing strategy is working. If after one year of implementing a promotion campaign you have no new sales, then it's time to hit the drawing board and derive a brand new strategy.

Now that you have developed a marketing campaign, you are ready to start increasing your contact list. The next step along the way is networking.

Network and Referral Based Marketing

The best way to promote your business and get ahead in your market is to join a business professional group. Almost every community across America has a local network of business professionals who come together to share thoughts and ideas. In other words, they are networking. *Networking* by definition is creating an interconnected system of things or people. When you reach out to other business professionals in your area, you're increasing your network and possibly increasing your client base.

The idea of networking is really simple: the more people we build relationships with, the more open we are to opportunities. You can ask any successful business owner how they got to be where they are, and almost everyone will say it was receiving an opportunity from someone they know. Below are some networking tips.

Networking Tips

- **Always talk to people no matter where you are.** Whether you are at a wedding, on an airplane, or in line at the post office, you never know who you can meet and what benefits that person can bring you. It pays to be courteous and strike up a conversation with others.
- **Stay in touch with the people you do know.** Don't let connections fall off the radar, stay in touch with the people already in your network. You don't need to talk every day, but an occasional call or email to touch base is always advised. Luckily these days, social networking sites make it easy to stay in touch with your contacts (we will discuss this later).
- **Always have something to offer.** There is nothing worse than someone who only wants to network to gain favors from others. You have a talent, a service and you may know someone who can help someone else. You can only receive when you give, so be prepared to offer assistance when you are seeking assistance.
- **Always have a business card on hand.** You never know when you may meet a potential client. Always have a business card or other promotional material on hand to offer when you meet new people.
- **Join any networking or professional association in your industry.** Part of becoming a recognized business is becoming recognized by other businesses in your industry. It is best to become a member of any and all professional business organizations locally, nationally and even internationally.

Most cities always have local chamber events going on. Check with your local Chamber of Commerce to see what business groups exist in your area. You can also go online to Business Networking International (BNI) which is an online business referral network for businesses all over the globe, (www.bni.com) or there's LeTip International, a Professional Business Leads Organization where members can gain from personal referrals (www.letip.com).

Using Social Media

Social Media encompasses a wide variety of Internet communication methods between people, including blogs, instant messaging, videos and social networking. People use social media to connect with current and new contacts and to communicate with others. By utilizing social media outlets, businesses can now keep in close contact with current and future consumers and stay in touch with people's wants and needs, while also promoting current and new products and services. In fact, you would be hard pressed to find a business today that doesn't have a profile on Facebook and Twitter. If you've never heard those terms before, then you are behind the times. Technology is changing almost daily, and it is the business that capitalizes on new trends that stays afloat.

These days, everyone (from kids to grandparents) is using the social networking sites we mentioned previously. No matter the age, these people are not only potential contacts, they are potential clients. By setting up social networking accounts for your business, you'll be doing a lot of free advertising, promotion, even client support. You'll also be expanding your social and professional network. Here are a few other benefits of using social media:

- Increase your online presence.
- Keep clients updated on news and events.
- You control the content.
- Receive feedback from satisfied and dissatisfied clients.
- An avenue for looking for new hires.
- It's FREE!

Below we will profile the many different social media sites you should be using when starting a new business.

Blogs, Social Networking & YouTube

A blog is nothing more than a web log, thus b-l-o-g. A blog is like an online diary, and can be either personal or business in nature. When a business utilizes a blog on their website, it can be a great tool in creating a more personal communication between you and your clients. Through your daily, weekly or monthly blog, you can share helpful tips on using your products or services, talk about advancements in the industry, share news about yourself and/or anyone who works for you, or just write about your feelings on business and the economy in general. YouTube on the other hand is a video sharing site.

YouTube (http://www.youtube.com)

LEARN MORE

http://authr.me/cJW

YouTube allows anyone to upload a short video to be shared with their online community. These videos can be viewed by anyone and are searchable through all online search engines. As a business, you can upload videos that will help promote your product or service. Best of all, posting onto YouTube is free. If you cannot afford the thousands of dollars to advertise on television, then YouTube is a great way to get a visual ad out about you and your new business. You will need to promote your video which is where social networking sites come in.

Facebook (http://www.facebook.com)

LEARN MORE

http://authr.me/cJX

Facebook is a social networking website where users can create home pages, search for people, and invite people to become their "friend" thereby becoming a part of their social network. As it is by invitation only, Facebook is a very popular site for people looking to keep up with close contacts. You can send your friends messages, share photos and video, or post a message directly to your wall (a type of homepage where friends can post messages for the user and other friends to see) for your entire friend list to read.

Facebook is currently the most used social networking site across the globe, with an estimated 400 million users.

It was when Facebook created fan pages in addition to personal pages that businesses started to take notice. A fan page is a public page where anyone can become a "fan" of the user. If you're a business, a fan page is a great way to accumulate dozens, hundreds or even thousands of current and potential clients in one place. The more people who become your fan, the more connected you can stay with an ever growing group of potential clients. Your fans can communicate directly with you or just follow your news and updates. Any posts you make to your fan page will not only spread to your fans, but also to *their* friends in their network; thus the power of social networking. And best of all, this service is free.

Twitter *(http://twitter.com)*

LEARN MORE

http://authr.me/cJY

Think of Twitter as a mini-blog. Twitter is a website that allows their users to post written updates of 140 characters or less; just enough space for a catchy sentence. These posts are called "tweets" and allow users to share news or personal thoughts with their followers. A follower is a user who chooses to keep updated on the tweets of other users. When you tweet, your followers will automatically get notice in their Twitter account, email account and even directly to their cell phone. What makes Twitter so pervasive is that anyone with a cell phone can link their text messaging service directly to their Twitter account so they can tweet and/or receive tweets in the form of a text message from their phones.

Essentially, Twitter is a way to publish information in small increments. By creating a Twitter account, you can keep all of your followers instantly updated with any news about your business or any sales or promotions that you have going on. Conversely, your followers can communicate directly with you, and can give you great insight into the minds of your clients. Twitter, like Facebook, is a fee service so it will cost you nothing to contact your clients, it only takes time. But since tweets are only a sentence or two, it doesn't even really take your time, either.

LinkedIn (*http://*www.linkedin.com)

LEARN MORE

http://authr.me/cJZ

Think of LinkedIn as Facebook for business professionals. LinkedIn is a social networking service geared towards business professionals to expand their network amongst other business professionals. It allows users to effectively network over the internet. LinkedIn has upwards of 40 million users and all of the businesses on the Forbes top 500 list can be found here. By communicating with others within and outside of your field, you can gain insight into the market and generate new ideas. It is also a great way to post a resume for yourself in case you decide to look for other work, and conversely, you can post job listings if you're looking to hire an employee.

LinkedIn has a homepage where users can post important facts about themselves and their business, as well as list their accomplishments. It's almost like creating an interactive business resume. You can also join groups with other like-minded entrepreneurs so you can keep an ongoing dialogue with others in a related field. LinkedIn has been a way for many business professionals to increase the number of their contacts, and to serve as an avenue for seeking out new and innovative ideas.

Google Plus (http://www.google.com/+)

Google Plus offers many of the same core features as Facebook. Instead of liking posts that others have made in Google Plus you Plus One (+1) it. But it is basically the same as liking something. Then when you want to add your friends you first create a circle (sub-group) to add them to if you do not already have a circle defined. Additionally, one very powerful tool from Google Plus offers a powerful tool called "Hang Outs" where you can organize sub-groups of 'friends' into live real-time video conferencing.

Social Media has never been more prevalent than it is today. The more people turn to the computer to stay connected with the world, the more imperative it is for businesses to have a strong online presence. There is no cost for you to start accounts with Twitter, Facebook, LinkedIn and Google Plus. Therefore, there is no reason for you not to use those sites to get the word out about your business. Since there is no cost associated, you are in reality gaining an opportunity for free marketing. Don't pass it up.

Finding Work by Bidding on Projects

Now that you know your talent, you have a service to offer, and your new business is set up, you can begin doing work. Sounds easy, but finding clients isn't always so easy. However, when looking to find work, the best place to look is on the internet. In the last few years, we've seen the rise of virtual marketplaces where employers hire freelancers for jobs over the internet versus in person.

When you work freelance, you can work for any number of employers on any number of jobs. Finding an employer is essentially finding a client, as you will be providing a service and be getting paid for that service. As a consultant, this means you can take on multiple clients while still being your own boss. Thanks to the internet, there are now multiple websites where you can search for employers to hire you.

Check out the freelance websites such as www.oDesk.com www.freelancer.com, and www.guru.com, as well as some specialty sites like www.rentacoder.com (for custom software) and www.crowdspring.com (for custom logo and graphic design). These websites offer an arena for freelancers to create a profile that showcases their talent and experience, and then bid on jobs by employers who are looking for remote workers. A *remote worker* is someone who works away from the main office or location where a business does its operations; can be an employee or a temporary hire.

When looking to freelance you are essentially looking to do a project for someone from your own business location. The internet has made it possible to do this quickly and efficiently. These freelance websites cover many types of services including writing, web and graphic design, computer IT services, software developers, client service representatives, engineering, administrative support, marketing and advertising professionals, and even consultants.

We will take a moment to go through these sites, offer up some pros and cons, talk about the cost, how you perform work and get paid, and give you a peek of what it looks like to create an account and start looking for work.

oDesk

ODesk is more like a virtual office than a freelancing marketplace. ODesk is designed for businesses (usually small ones) to look for virtual workers who they can hire on an hourly basis and monitor the work they are doing through the website. From an employer's perspective, you can use oDesk to search for qualified business professionals who you would like to add to your "team". You can hire them remotely, assign jobs and tasks, monitor their daily output, and authorize weekly payments. You can choose to hire someone long-term or short-term.

From an employee perspective, oDesk is an opportunity to search for regular and steady work from an employer who has a need that you are able to fulfill. You will be able to work from home, or from your own office, while having the guarantee of steady work. As you work, your time is logged through the website, and you can easily invoice and receive payment through the website as well. As a consultant, oDesk can be a good way to gain some regular employment.

You can create an account on oDesk as either a provider, meaning you are a professional looking to get hired for your particular talent, or as an employer who is posting a job. Providers can be independent contractors, or businesses that provide certain services. There is no fee to join oDesk as either an employer or provider, however oDesk takes 10% of the posted rates that are paid by employers. This means, if you are a freelancer who is asking to get paid $9 an hour, the employer will end up paying $10 an hour, with $1 going to oDesk.

Freelancer.com and Guru.com

Freelancer.com and Guru.com are freelance marketplaces where employers post projects and accept bids from qualified freelancers. This is usually done on a project-by-project basis, with employment only lasting as long as the project takes to complete. When a bid is accepted, the employer and freelancer make a project agreement that sets the timeline and the price. Once the project is complete, the freelancer invoices the employer, who then sends payment through the website. Even though they are slightly different in how they set up their interface, they both basically offer the same service. Both websites are free to join, yet they do take a project fee from all earnings freelancers make (usually between 5%-10%).

Freelancer.com (http://www.freelancer.com) is a global freelance marketplace for freelancers from all manner of industries, including graphic designers, software engineers, computer programmers, writers, as well as marketing and advertising professionals. Employers can hire a freelancer for a project, and then submit payment through the website. Freelancer takes a percentage from the earnings of freelancers, and also charges employers a commission when a freelancer is hired. It is free to create a profile, however there is a fee if you choose to upgrade to Gold Member status. Being a Gold Member allows you to pay the website a smaller fee from your earnings, and Gold Member employers do not have to pay a commission when they hire a freelancer. The website has a system of rating both employers and freelancers based on performance, and this rating system helps users gain more recognition on the site.

Guru.com (http://www.guru.com) is another online virtual marketplace where employers can search for temporary freelancers. Guru has professionals from a number of industries whether business, technology or the creative arts. It is free to have a basic freelancer profile on guru, however your search and bidding options are limited. For a yearly fee, freelancers can upgrade their account to "Guru" status from "basic" status, which allows them to search and bid on more projects than a basic member. Also as a Guru member, you will pay a slightly smaller project fee from your earnings. Guru currently has over 1 million users worldwide, and is the largest online marketplace for freelancers. Freelancers are rated on their performance as well as the feedback they have received from past employers.

The good news about these websites is they do offer a certain level of protection to freelancers in regards to receiving payments from employers. Though not always guaranteed, Freelancer and Guru may try to mediate between the two parties if a dispute arises. Guru offers an Escrow service, where for a fee of 7%-12% of the project total, you can require an employer to deposit the full amount due for the project into an escrow account before the project begins. The money will stay in the escrow account until the employer authorizes the release to the freelancer. This assures you that an employer is serious about payment before you do any work. Freelancer offers the same type of service through their Milestone Payments System. Both services offer dispute resolution if a problem arises. It's a safer way to work, though you are paying for it.

The drawback, however, to these sites is the fierce competition that exists between freelancers. Some jobs can have upwards of 50 project bids, which tends to mean the job gets awarded to the lowest bidder. Although not all of the time, but underbidding does occur, and it always hurts the community as a whole. When working through a website such as Freelancer or Guru it is advisable to be honest about the value you offer to an employer. Though it can take time to search and bid on projects, the most qualified freelancers always end up working the most.

Secondly, make sure you are aware of all of the fees that each sites imposes upon payments. These sites make money by taking a percentage of the total fee paid to freelancers by employers, and it can vary anywhere between 5% - 10% which comes out of the freelancers' earnings. Freelancer.com also charges employers a 3% commission when they choose a freelancer. Make sure to read the fine print about any fees and charges associated with working through these websites, and budget that into your rates.

vWorker (formerly RentACoder) and Crowdspring

vWorker (http://www.vworker.com) is a virtual marketplace where businesses can hire virtual computer programmers on either a project or short-term basis. Because the work is done over the internet, businesses can now span the globe looking for the best computer programmers for the best price. The site has recently expanded to include graphic designers, writers, translators, as well as any other number of professionals. Funds are not paid to freelancers directly, but instead to an escrow account through the vWorker website. vWorker takes a 15% fee from the money paid to the coder, so make sure you keep this percentage in mind when setting your rates. If payment disputes occur, vWorker will attempt to resolve the problem between the parties.

CrowdSpring (http://www.crowdspring.com) is a website for mostly custom logo and graphic designers to find work, however there are also freelance writers who use the site. It is set up as a virtual marketplace where employers can find the creative talent they need to help with their design from anywhere in the US or around the world. This site works pretty much the same as other freelancing sites, though slightly more personalized. Employers post projects detailing what they want and a deadline. Freelancers, who they call "creatives", then submit their design and/or written work for that project. The employer selects which work they like, and can work with the creative to revise the design until the employer is satisfied. There is no actual bidding. The site also provides employers a legal contract for free that guarantees that the employer is the sole owner of the work. Now for the creatives, this means you are doing work with no guarantee of being selected or being paid. However, it is a great avenue to get your creative work seen if you are a designer or creative writer.

There has never been a better time to find lucrative work over the internet as a freelancer. Best of all, this means entrepreneurs can save overhead costs by working from anywhere they want, even their own homes. You just need a good computer and reliable internet access.

In Conclusion

In this chapter, we have discussed ways for you to find, reach and obtain new clients for your consulting business. We have talked about the importance of marketing and how to create a marketing strategy. We have also talked about networking and why making relationships with other consultants and business professionals is a priority. We then learned about the importance of social media, and provided a list of websites you need to become a member of to further your business. Lastly, we talked about the many project bidding websites that are marketplaces for employers to find and hire temporary freelancers.

In the next chapter, we will talk about growth and the many ways you can take your consulting business to the next level.

Before moving on, however, we will take a moment to guide you step-by-step through the process of setting up an account as a freelancer on the project bidding site Guru.

How-To-Guide For Freelancers Via Guru

For the purposes of instruction, we will now take you through starting up a Guru.com account, creating a profile, and bidding on projects. We will discuss the necessary steps for the website for each step. It will be useful for you to be in front of a computer as you proceed through this section

How To Set Up A Guru Freelancer Account

1. **Open Account**. To open an account you need to first go to www.guru.com and in the top right hand corner of the page hit the tab labeled "Register". The next screen will prompt you to either register as an employer or register as a freelancer. Choose Freelancer.

2. **Registration**. Next on the registration screen, you will need to fill in all of your information such as name and contact information, desired screen name, account username and password, your email preferences, and then you must agree to the Terms of Service and Privacy Policy. When done, hit Register.

3. **Area of Expertise**. After registration, you will be directed through a series of prompts to begin your account. First, you need to choose an area of expertise, and the list is quite exhaustive.

4. **Subcategories**. Next you will choose up to 5 subcategories that further describe what it is that you do.

5. **Membership**. The last part of the setup process asks what type of membership you require. You can use Guru at the 'basic' level for free, however, Guru does offer upgraded memberships at a yearly price ranging from $100 - $350 that you can either pay quarterly or annually. Paying money to upgrade is well worth the cost. An upgraded Guru membership will allow you to search and bid on any project you choose, where basic members are limited to projects that fit within their

profile. Basic members are also limited to 10 bids a month, while Guru members can bid on up to 100 projects a month. An upgraded membership also means you will pay a much lower percentage to the website out of your earnings (5% instead of 10%).

6. **Profile Page**. Now that you have set up your guru account, you will be directed to your profile page. Here you will see many options. To the right is the profile monitor, letting you know how much of the profile process you have completed. To have a profile that provides enough information for employers looking to hire you, you will want to fill in more information. Here is the information you will need to complete: Screen identity, uploaded resume, any images you wish to add, a brief overview of your qualifications and experience, and any work samples you can upload.

   A basic membership allows for 10 bids at one time. When you bid on a project, you are using an available bid. Once the project you have bid on chooses a professional or closes, you will receive another bid in its place. Guru allows you to purchase more bids for a fee.

7. **Overview Tab**. Before you start bidding on projects, you will want to hit Overview on the right hand side of your profile. This will allow you to fill in more important information before you begin working on the site. You will need to set your minimum rate per hour, your minimum project bid, and whether or not you will work onsite. The other tabs allow you to fill in any career highlights, important skills you possess, and more specific work terms you want to enter (such as payment terms, turnaround times, communication methods, etc.).

8. **My Account**. Now that you have filled in your profile, you will want to hit the My Account tab on the top left of the screen. This will take you to your Account Home Page. It is here you can search for projects, track projects you have bid on, access the work room where you can talk to your employer and upload any documents, and also see your account balance.

Congratulations. You have now set up your freelance Guru account. Next, we will walk you through searching for projects, placing bids, accepting projects, working with the employer through the website's interface, and then invoicing.

How To Bid and Work On Projects on Guru

1. **Search for projects**. Under the Get Work tab you will select Search for Projects. On the screen select your area of expertise, for example, Business Consulting.

2. **Browse Posted Projects**. Now you will see a list of posted projects by employers, with the most recent projects listed first. You can sort the results any number of ways, and can even refine your search by sub-categories. Every project has a project ID, as well as a Title, the Main Category they go under, as well as the relevant skills needed for the project. There is also a Budget range (if one is posted) that the employer is seeking. Then you can view the Employer Statistics so you know their track record as far as number of projects posted, number accepted and number of invoices paid, as well as their rating from past freelancers. This will let you know if an employer is serious or not. Finally, you can see the number of days available to bid on the project, as well as if the project is open for bidding or closed (invite only).

3. **View project**. When you select a project, you will be able to view more details. It is here you check out statistics on the employer. Secondly, check out their proposed budget as well as the specifics of what they are looking for. For our example, our sample Employer Entrepreneur Boot Camp Publishing has posted a project and invited our freelancer to place a bid.

NOTE: Employers can seek out qualified freelancers and "invite" them to bid on their projects. If you have received a project invitation, you will be notified by email and also on your home page at guru.com.

4. **Submit Proposal.** If you have determined that you would like to place a bid on the project, then hit the button on the bottom called Submit Proposal. You will then be guided through a series of screens to place your monetary bid and outline your proposal. The following screen shots take you through the process of submitting a proposal, then confirming the details before the bid is sent to the employer. It will cost you one bid to submit a proposal. Basic members can submit 10 bids a month, while Guru members can submit 100. A *Premium* proposal will cost 10 bids. It is a signal to the employer that you are serious about their project and feel strongly that you can be of service.

5. **Project Tracker Alert: Awarded Project**. If you have been selected for the project by the employer, you will receive a notice, called an Alert, under you Project Tracker Tab. The Project Tracker Tab allows you to track the projects you have bid on, as well as the projects you have been awarded.

6. **Accept Project Award and Define Project Agreement**. After you have been selected, you can click on the awarded project to review the bid you placed. If you are still comfortable with those terms, you hit the button at the bottom of the screen titled Accept Project Award. You will then be asked to upload a project agreement and define your terms (meaning when you'll be paid). It is good to have your contract in a Word document that you can upload into the system. This, along with your payment terms, will be sent to the employer for approval. Guru allows you to set milestones as well as the final date of delivery. This is a way for you to set up incremental payments and milestone deadlines, or you can have everything due at the final due date. Make your choice, and then send to the employer for approval.

7. **Begin Project**. After you have received another notification that the employer has accepted your project agreement, you can begin work. It will be between the employer and you how you will communicate and deliver work product. You can either do your own personal email, or communicate through the Guru website. Guru has a Private Database feature where you can post messages between you and your employer. There's also a Work Room where you can upload documents onto the Guru Server for the employer to then download and review.

8. **Invoice Employer Upon Completion**. After you have performed your duties and have given the final deliverable, it will be up to you to invoice the employer through Guru. Guru has two methods: SafePay Invoicing and SafePay Escrow. The Escrow service is more secure, yet there is a fee involved (2% of total project). For Escrow, the employer is required to pay the total amount due for the project upfront into an Escrow account that Guru manages. Once the money is there, you begin work and the employer authorizes the release of funds either upon completion or a pre-determined time. Guru will help moderate any disputes of payment with this service. Guru's basic SafePay Invoicing is a way for you to send the employer an invoice and have them pay you directly through Guru. There is no protection, but you can withdraw funds from your Guru Account directly to your bank account with no additional charge.

   Under your Project Tracker Tab you can select Submit Invoice. From here, you will be prompted through a series of screens to enter in the amount as well as a description of services.

9. **Manage Payments & Feedback**. After you have been paid by the employer, you can manage your account. On your My Account page you will see the section called Manage Payments & Feedback. It is here where you can choose the method you want to withdraw your funds, as well as offer your employer feedback. Be

sure to ask your employer to give you feedback as well. Guru employs a ratings system for freelancers and employers, and the more positive ratings you acquire, the better chance you have for being picked for future projects.

There you have it, a step-by-step guide to working with Guru. For instructions on how to access Guru as an Employer, turn to the Employer section in the next chapter.

Achieving Growth

In this chapter, we will talk about growth: how to plan for growth, how to work towards growth, and how to accommodate growth. We will talk about the concept of outsourcing, and how to be an effective manager. Lastly, we will revisit freelance project bidding websites, but this time from the viewpoint of an employer looking to hire others. By the end of this chapter, you will understand:

- How to move from being a startup to being a growing business
- The normal life cycle of a business
- How to expand your business by outsourcing
- How to manage others
- How to use project bidding sites as an employer

Moving from Startup to Growing Business

Every new business has a life cycle and that cycle always will include a stage for growth. No startup business stays a true startup forever. The fact is that businesses that do not grow will eventually fail. Below is a brief overview of the natural life cycle for any business structure.

Business Life Cycle

1. **Birth of a new idea**. All new businesses start with a new idea for a product or service. During this stage, a new idea is formed, a business plan is created, financing is procured, and the idea takes form as a new business.
2. **Start-up**. The startup phase is when the actual business is physically formed, the product or service is introduced into the market, and customers are acquired. The biggest concern during this phase is the management of cash and the ability to begin to make a profit.
3. **Growth**. Once a business has started operations, growth is required. This stage represents the first change in strategy needed for a new business. The focus shifts to increasing sales as well as expanding operations. This is also where the emergence of other competitors takes place.
4. **Stabilization**. Following growth, most businesses will naturally experience a slowdown in activity. A business will often toggle between growth and stabilization. However, a business should not stay in a stable period for very long. A slowdown in sales usually signals a need to reinvent and invigorate the business.
5. **Expansion or Death**. There will come a time for every business where they either have to change or die. Change can be the sale of the business to a bigger company or expansion into new markets or geographic territories. A business that does not eventually change cannot survive in the long run.

For the purposes of this chapter, we will be focusing on moving from the second stage of the life cycle to the third stage which is growth. Once you have successfully completed the startup phase of your business, it will be time to look towards growth and there are many different steps a business can take to expand.

Do not make the mistake of being happy with the status quo. A business needs to have a steady influx of new clients in order to be able to survive in the long run, especially in the consulting business. Consultants will always have a mix of repeat clients and one-time only clients. By not taking concerted steps to bring in new business, a consultant can easily run out of contacts, and clients, within a few years. By placing a high priority on growing your business, you will ensure that your business exits the startup phase and becomes a successful long-term business. And this priority needs to exist from the very beginning.

The minute you begin doing business, you need to start planning for growth. Sometimes creating a strategy to grow a company is as simple as changing your perceptions of opportunity. The following are some practices that can be adopted to help promote future growth.

Growth Strategies

1. **Develop and introduce a new product or service.** The easiest way to grow is 'horizontally', by developing and introducing new products or services into the marketplace. For single owner operations this may not be feasible, but if you can expand upon what you already offer, even by just changing a specification or adding a new skill, you will have something new to market. When you have something new to offer, you can not only gain new clients, but you can keep current clients coming back.

2. **Expand into new markets or territories.** The internet is the quickest and easiest way to expand your current client base. By participating in e-

commerce and selling your products or services over the internet, you can expand outside your community and reach potential clients across the nation, even across the globe.

3. **Go Global.** To expand even further upon point number 2, you can easily expand your client base by selling to clients in other countries. Thanks to the internet, selling goods and services in other countries is fairly easy and fairly profitable. This will require more market research on your part to determine if there is a need for your product or service, and what regulations and fees you might face.

4. **Hire employees or outsource.** Growth will mean more business, and more business will eventually mean you need to hire help. There's only so much work in one week that a single person can do. But a dozen people can accomplish much more. However, having staff will require an increase in overhead costs such as office space as well as other fixed costs such as salaries. For small businesses, outsourcing jobs has allowed them to effectively hire help without having to hire and house full-time employees. We will talk about outsourcing in more detail in the next section.

5. **Create a strategic alliance.** A *strategic alliance* is a business relationship between two or more entities for mutual gain. By finding other businesses in a similar and related field and partnering up, you can expand your reach in the local, national and even global community. You don't want to turn to other businesses you are competing against, but instead businesses where you have a similar client base and can benefit from the increased reach. For instance, if you are an event planner, you can partner with make-up artists, stylists and even different hotels and restaurants for cross marketing and promotions.

All businesses need to have growth strategies in place from the very beginning so they do not fall into a rut. There are only so many family, friends and acquaintances you can turn to before you have exhausted your contact list and need to begin bringing in new clients.

So how will you know you are growing and thriving as a consultant? Below is a simple list of characteristics of successful and growing businesses.

Signs of a growing consulting business:
- A majority of your business is from referrals and clients finding you versus you actively pursuing new clients
- A large proportion of your clients are repeat clients
- You are able to be picky about accepting projects or jobs, and can turn down work without threatening your profit
- You have a clearly identifiable brand and you have a strong online presence (through your website, social media sites, as well as a top listing on any number of search engines)
- You have time to give back to the community and take on leadership positions in your industry (as we'll discuss in chapter 6)

As good as growth is for a business, a business will fail if it is not prepared to handle growth. If a young business grows too fast, they can find themselves with more demand for products and services than they are able to supply. However, if you are able to find ways to make money with little effort then this is not a problem. Next we will talk about growing your profits through passive income.

Create Some Passive Income

After you have put in the work to obtain clients and create some real income, it's time to look for some ways to bring in a passive income. *Passive Income* is money that is consistently received from products and/or services without any effort being put into obtaining it. The idea of receiving money with no effort may seem like a fairy tale, but the truth is it is quite possible. When you have developed a name for you and your business, then there are many ways you can use your notoriety and experience to generate further income, without having to spend large amounts of your time.

If you feel you have enough knowledge and expertise that others would be willing to pay for, then perhaps you might consider writing a book. Books, and e-books (electronic books sold over the internet) are popular and lucrative ways to use your skills to bring in more money. However, the list of ways to generate passive income includes more than just books. Here are some examples of ways that you, as a consultant, can generate passive income.

Passive Income for Consultants
- Books and e-books
- Pamphlets, manuals and training manuals
- Online articles
- Newsletters
- Speaking engagements, seminars and conferences
- Teleconferences and video podcasts
- Self-help audiotapes and videos
- Licensing and retailing your methods or practices
- Private coaching

Now, just because you can write a book doesn't mean it will easily sell. The market is currently flooded with experts giving how-to advice. The key is to have something relevant to say. Just as your unique talents make you perfectly suited to be a consultant, that uniqueness is what you must bring to any published material you create, as well as any speaking engagements. Below are some pointers for standing out in the crowd when looking to publish your material or create a speech.

Pointers for creating relevant material:

- **Have a unique point-of-view.** Don't say what hundreds of other consultants are saying. Try to focus on what you can offer that is different than everyone else and use that as your hook (what is relevant).

- **Encompass a wide consumer base**. The more limited your scope, the more limited your earning potential. Even though you have a specific niche as a consultant, try to think globally when wanting to deliver a message. Think of ways your expertise can help anyone, whether or not they are in your field.
- **Don't date yourself**. Try to avoid using points and examples that only apply to the current state of things. If you use dated examples, then your material will only be relevant for a short time. Try to encompass all economic and social situations.
- **Accept credit cards**. It is very easy to accept credit card payments online. Anyone these days can do it, especially with a service like PayPal. By not accepting credit cards, you are closing yourself off to a large portion of the consumer base.
- **Only do what is convenient for you**. Passive income is a great benefit when you have to put in the least amount of effort. If you are doing speaking engagements and coaching sessions, then do only what is convenient for you, where it is convenient. What would be ideal is if you could do your sessions from your own office, or by teleconference or internet podcast. Whatever you choose to do, make it easy.

Passive income is a great way to grow your profits without having to grow your operations. After the initial work of writing a book or manual, for example, you can continually receive profits on a regular basis. However, before you undertake an effort for passive income, it is best to make sure there is a market and/or demand for your service. Next, we will discuss another way to handle growth without spending a lot of money, and that is to outsource.

The Benefits of Outsourcing

Outsourcing has different definitions for different industries. For our purposes, we will say *outsourcing* is the contracting out of specified services to an outside provider.

> **Virtual Employee / Remote Worker**
> An individual that regularly works away from the main office or location where a business normally holds its operations.

Contracting work out to a third party has grown immensely in the last decade, mostly due to the rise of technologies that allow individuals to work for anyone from anywhere. Thanks to the internet and cell phone, we can communicate with others across the globe as easily as if we were in the same room.

Nowadays, an employee does not need to come to a physical location when they can turn in assignments over the internet. We call these workers *virtual employees* or *remote workers.*

What this means for small businesses is that they can save money on overhead costs while still reaping the benefit of a support staff. But there's an even greater advantage to utilizing remote workers: it becomes far easier to hire help *only when you need it* versus spending the money to hire a full-time employee.

As a consultant, there will come a time when you have more clients to service than hours to service them. It is a great problem to have, however you cannot risk a decrease in the quality of your service. For most consultants, this period of growth signals the need for support staff. When looking to save money (especially if you are working from a home office) hiring a remote employee on a temporary basis not only saves you money, it saves you time.

> **Temporary worker**
> An employee brought in on a short-term basis for a specified period of time or for a specified project. When the project or time period ends, so does the employment. Also called a temp, freelancer, contractual employee or seasonal employee.

Before we go into the many benefits of outsourcing your work to temporary workers, let us define the term temporary worker.

For the sake of simplicity, we will refer to these individuals as freelancers. When starting a new business, and even growing a new business, there are many benefits to relying on short-term freelancers instead of full-time employees. Below are some of the many benefits of outsourcing to freelancers.

Specific Benefits of Outsourcing:

- Freelancers are available to start right away.
- Freelancers have a specific area of expertise that you can utilize without any training needed.
- Freelancers can provide a skill that you lack.
- A freelance or temporary employee can free you up to focus on what you do best instead of spending your time doing menial tasks.
- You avoid having to formally hire or fire employees.
- You do not have to pay their taxes or any employee benefits. Freelancers work as independent contractors and therefore are responsible for their own taxes and benefits.
- They are temporary! Employment only lasts as long as you want or need.

People outsource for different reasons. As a consultant, bringing in help can actually allow you to take on more work; either by hiring on another expert in an area of expertise that you lack so that you can offer a more comprehensive service, or by hiring temporary employees to offer support for simple business tasks such as research, writing and editing of documents so you can focus on bringing your skills to the project at hand.

We cannot all be experts in everything. Still, you became a consultant in the first place because you have a specific skill and expertise to offer others. By bringing on temporary hires for specific projects, you can expand to include their expertise as part of your consulting services.

In the end, it is up to you how you would like to outsource your work. However, once you do bring on board an employee, even a temporary one, you are now taking on a new role – that of a manager.

Being a Manager

To use a broad definition, *management* is the organization and coordination of business activities and individuals to achieve a set of goals. An enormous part of managing is not only overseeing processes, but overseeing people. When you take on an employee, even a temporary one, you are now going to be responsible for overseeing their work product. You are officially a manager.

Here are some common functions of a manager:
- Set goals and expectations
- Plan and delegate tasks
- Communicate with employees what is expected of them
- Oversee processes
- Evaluate overall performance

When you bring on employees, you are bringing on the responsibility of managing their work flow. No matter how you look at it, when you hire others, you are taking on the role of a manager and it is not a role anyone should take lightly. For your business to thrive, you will need your employees, full-time or short-term, to work to the best of their ability in an efficient and timely manner. Below are some traits that a good manager must look to possess.

The best managers will seek to incorporate the following traits:

- Respect for others
- An ability to be open-minded
- Always seek to learn something new
- Allow for failure and reward creativity
- Seek to energize and encourage others to do their best

As a new business, you will most likely be looking to hire temporary workers, or freelancers, in the beginning so as to keep your costs low. Even so, you will be responsible for assigning them tasks and overseeing their work. This will most likely also mean they will be remote employees, working from their own office location versus yours. Implementing strategies to keep these temporary remote workers connected and working efficiently is therefore of the utmost importance. Below is a step-by-step guide to managing your remote workers.

Guide to Managing Remote Workers

1. **Stay connected**. You will need to use technology to stay connected to your freelancers and remote workers. Luckily, there are numerous ways you can communicate with your employees: internet, instant messaging and video chat to name a few. Make sure you are using all of them on a regular basis.

2. **Create a team spirit**. If you are in the position of hiring more than one worker for a project, then you will need to foster a team spirit amongst your workers. It will benefit you and your workers if everyone feels they are a part of a team working towards a common goal. Especially when your workers are remote. Working outside of an office setting can be isolating. To help foster a community spirit, you will not only need to stay in contact with your workers, you will need to encourage them to connect with each other. Involve teams on group emails, group chats and group phone conferences. Set up virtual meetings where everyone can discuss what they're doing. Make sure everyone knows what the goals are and what everyone else is doing to meet those goals.

3. **Establish guidelines for communications**. These days the use of cell phones, email, and text messaging means you can communicate with others any hour of the day. However, that doesn't mean you *should*. As soon as you bring on a freelancer or employee, it is

wise to set a guideline for communicating. Establish regular hours for personal communications such as when you are available by phone or by instant message. Secondly, establish what modes are good for certain types of communications. If employees have problems or concerns, then you need to have a verbal communication. If you are just checking in on progress, you can do an email. Let all of your workers know what you expect and then you can better manage your regular communications.

4. **Focus on the end result, not the method**. The good news about remote workers is that, generally speaking, they are fairly independent and need little supervision. The drawback is that as a manger you will not be able to supervise everything. Yes, you will be assigning tasks, but you will not be able to control the manner in which the task is done; you can only judge the result. If the results are not meeting expectations, then you may need to meet with your remote worker to go over their methods. Otherwise, you will need to evaluate performance based on what is turned in to you directly.

5. **Always offer support**. Remote workers will need more encouragement than those employees you see on a regular basis because they do not have the benefit of consistent and personalized feedback. Make sure to always check in with your remote workers, look at the work they are doing and offer your guidance.

Regardless of whether your employees, temporary or permanent, are just outside your office or across the country, you will need to be a constant presence in their daily work activities.

Being a manager is rewarding yet challenging. Effectively managing others is not a task anyone can take nonchalantly. If you are looking to expand your business to the point where you will eventually be staffing an office, then it is suggested you take an in-depth look at managing and everything that the duty entails. Check out **The Certified Entrepreneur Program: Management Training Manual** offered by Guanzi Institute.

In Conclusion

In this chapter, we have talked about taking your business from a startup to a growing and thriving business. We have talked about the typical life cycle of a business and have outlined the need for all businesses to grow. We listed some growth strategies you need to employ and discussed the idea of outsourcing your work. We also talked about the benefits of utilizing remote employees. Lastly, we talked about becoming a manager, and how to efficiently manage your workers.

In the final chapter, we will talk about the need for joining a consulting industry organization, and why you should look to donating your services as a way of giving back to your community.

But first, we will provide you with a step-by-step guide to finding a freelance worker through the project bidding site Guru.com.

How-To-Guide For Employers Via Guru

For the purposes of instruction, we will now take you through starting up a Guru.com account as an employer looking to hire freelancers. We will take you through creating a profile, listing a project and accepting bids. We will discuss the necessary steps for each step.

How-To Set Up A Guru Employer Account and Post Projects

1. **Open Account**. To open an account you need to first go to www.guru.com and in the top right hand corner of the page hit the tab labeled "Register". The next screen will prompt you to either register as an Employer or register as a Freelancer. Choose Employer.

2. **Registration**. Next on the registration screen, you will need to fill in all of your information such as name and contact information, desired screen name, account username and password, your email preferences, and then you must agree to the Terms of Service and Privacy Policy. When done hit Register.

3. **Home Screen**. After you have registered, you will be directed to your Home Screen. Here you can Post Projects, Track your posted projects, Post and Review any messages, as well as see your Employment Statistics – including how many projects you have posted, how many freelancers you have selected and how many invoices you have paid.

4. **Post a Project**. Next, you will want to post a project. To post, hit Post A Project on the top right of your Home Screen. You will then be directed through a series of screens where you can define and refine your terms.

   a. **Main Skill**. The first screen will ask for you to select a Main Skill Category, which is basically defining what industry your project applies to. For example, Business Consulting.

b. **Primary Skill**. After choosing the main category, you will need to select a primary skill or specialty for your category. For example Business Planning.

c. **Project Details**. Next you will need to fill in the specific details of your project, including the title, a description of your needs, and your estimated budget range. You can also upload any files that you feel are necessary to share with freelancers. You will then need to refine your skill requirements. For example Business Planning and E-Business Management. Lastly, you need to state where the work needs to be done, whether it's in a specific location or not. If you are hiring a remote worker who will work with you over the internet, choose No Location Requirements.

Then, you need to state whether or not you want your posting to be Public or Private. Public will be viewed by anyone on Guru. Private means you plan on inviting specific freelancers to bid on your project and you do not want your project bid on by all members. The final screen will let you confirm all the details before you click on Post Project Now!

5. **Invite Freelancers to Bid**. If you chose to have a Private listing, you will now need to search for freelancers to bid on your project. You will be taken to a Search Screen where you can either browse freelancers by category, or you can search for a freelancer name. We have searched for "freelancer" and found our freelancer who we would like to invite. After selecting the freelancer, you can decide whether or not to invite them to a new project, or your existing project. Finally, you will get confirmation our invitation was sent.

View Quotes. When a freelancer submits a quote on your project, you will be notified via email as well as your Home Screen at Guru.com. From your home page, you can go to your Project Manager Screen where you can browse quotes in order to make a selection.

6. **Award Project**. Once you have chosen a freelancer to work with, you can officially award them the project. A notification will be sent to the freelancer, and they can accept the award or decline it. When you choose to award the project, you will be asked whether or not you want to stop the bidding on your project, or allow more freelancers to bid.

7. **Accept Project Agreement**. After the freelancer has accepted the project, you will see the project in your Project Manager Tab. Here you can monitor progress, post announcements or questions through a private database, and also see uploaded files by the freelancer in a private Work Room. The freelancer will also send you a Project Agreement that contains the contract as well as their terms for payment. You will need to look this over and accept, decline or send requested revisions to the freelancer. Once accepted, the work will begin.

8. **Pay Invoice when Project Complete**. After the project is complete, the freelancer will send you an invoice through Guru's SafePay Invoice System (unless they choose the Escrow Service which we'll talk about below). You will get a notification in the Manage Payments & Feedback section of your Home Page. Here you can review the Invoice, and then select Pay. You can pay by credit card, PayPal, check, E-check, or wire transfer. You can also pay with funds you have transferred into your SafePay Account. Guru has a promotion that will give you "Loyalty Dollars" when you use check, E-check, wire transfer or your SafePay Account. This can equal up to 2% of your payment. Guru's Escrow Service: the employer is required to pay the total amount due for the project upfront into an Escrow account that Guru manages. Once the money is there, the freelancer begins work and you authorize

the release of funds either upon completion or a pre-determined time. The best benefit to the service is that you only release funds when you are satisfied with your deliverable. Guru will also help moderate any disputes of payment with this service.

That's all there is to using Guru as an employer. Having the ability to post projects and receive quotes from freelancers will give you the best chance of choosing the most qualified individual for the best price.

Get Involved With Your Community

In this chapter, we will discuss why and how you should use your consulting skills to give back to your community. We will talk about the many different consulting organizations you can join, as well as how to use your success to make a difference for others. By the end of this chapter, you will understand:

- The consulting industry organizations you should belong to and how they function
- How to get involved with your local community
- Why consulting puts you in a perfect position to help others

Consulting Industry Organizations You Need to Contact

When you work as a consultant, you are in the position to give aid and assistance to others based on your unique talents. In addition, you will be creating a name for yourself as a service provider. The best way to ensure that your name is well circulated is to become a visible presence within your local community as well as within the virtual community over the internet. Sure, the more satisfied clients you have, the more your name will spread. But you also need to take the initiative and join a number of consulting organizations where you can not only network with others, but create a name for yourself through the many activities the organization carries out.

Now, just as there are many different types of consultants, there are also many different types of consulting organizations. There simply is not enough space or time available to list them all. However, below is a varied list of many prominent consulting organizations and what they do.

Consulting Organizations

The following list of consulting organizations will give you an idea of what's available for different sections of the consulting industry. First, we will list the general organizations that cover a wide variety of consultants followed by a short list of industry specific organizations.

The Association of Professional Consultants (http://www.consultapc.org)

The Association of Professional Consultants (APC) is a referral organization that allows visitors to search a list of qualified and certified consultants to fit their needs. The APC covers a broad range of consulting services, including finance, coaching, human resources, information technology (IT), management, marketing and advertising, manufacturing, sales and business development, and training, among many other specialties. Members of the Association receive many benefits besides being listed on the online community, such as member referrals, networking event opportunities, as well as the ability to learn from your consulting peers. Check out their website for membership details and the qualifications that are required.

Professional and Technical Consultants Association (http://www.patca.org)

PATCA is another professional of association of consultants that covers over 200 areas of expertise. PATCA is a non-profit organization that is run by consultants that offers networking opportunities for its members, as well as a free referral service. As a member, you can obtain new business leads, expand your client base, receive some marketing help, and get a boost to your consulting credibility. Also, individuals and businesses can post projects to the site so that member consultants can offer proposals.

Industry Specific Organizations

Institute of Management Consultants, USA (http://www.imcusa.org)

The IMC, USA organization is a member-only organization that seeks to enhance the public profile of management consultants from across the United States by promoting ethics and excellence through certification and education. All members have a profile on the website that is searchable by visitors looking to find a management consultant in their area. The organization also has several regional chapters, where members can attend local networking events.

Independent Computer Consultant Association (http://www.icaa.org)

The ICCA is a directory of computer and IT consulting professionals. The organization serves as a place where consultants can network with one another and reach out for support, as well as a forum where individuals and businesses can seek out qualified advice from the independent network of computer experts.

Tech Serve Alliance (http://www.techservealliance.org)

This Alliance is an association of Information Technology (IT) businesses, consultants and providers that offer a collaborative networking and information-sharing service for members. They are the gateway for businesses to keep up to date on what's happening in the IT industry, including technological advances as well as any congressional rulings. They also provide a searchable online directory of members.

Human Resources Consultants Association (http://www.hrca.com)

The HRCA is a professional association for Human Resources consultants, whether individuals or consulting firms. They offer a searchable database of qualified HR consultants to help start-ups with staffing strategies including hiring and benefits plans. The site also allows companies to post for a job opening or consulting need to which members can respond.

Association of Image Consultants International (http://www.aici.org)

The AICI is the place for Image consultants to not only become certified through the organization's certification process, but to also network with other image consultants and gain visibility by being a listed member on their website. Image consulting is a rising industry that can aid an individual or business with their physical appearance, behavior and communication skills.

Qualitative Research Consultants Association (http://www.qrca.org)

QRCA is a listing of consultants that offer information for businesses looking to obtain market research and consumer habit information. A Qualitative Research consultant is one who can provide information that businesses seek through data accumulation, focus groups, surveys and other observational research. The organization has local chapters, as well as an online directly so members can network with each other and pool their resources and information.

As stated earlier, this is only a partial list of consulting organizations. Be sure to also check your local community as well as within your industry to see what organizations are available to fit your specific niche.

Giving Back to Your Community

Hopefully, you will reach a point in your consulting career where you are making enough of a profit to consider your consulting endeavor a success. What now? Sure, you want to keep growing and keep raking in money. But there is something to be said for using success to give back to your community. "Giving back to your community," is a way of asking you to make a difference by donating your time and expertise for free. Giving free services is a form of donation, only you are donating time instead of money. You get paid for your expertise and skills as a consultant, so by donating those skills to benefit your community you are, in essence, giving back.

By participating in local non-profit organizations, either as a founder, board member or volunteer, you can provide your services to others. *Non-profit organizations* are organizations that do not distribute any surplus funds to members or shareholders, but instead use those funds to realize their goals. A non-profit, or NPO is usually set-up to enhance the local community, or offer as educational or public service. They can be religious organizations, social welfare organizations, professional trade associations (like your local Chamber of Commerce) or charities created to serve a specific cause.

These organizations function like a business, which means they have needs just like regular businesses. If you are a consultant, providing your expertise to these organizations for free is not only a way to increase your public profile, but you'll be helping a good cause in the process. Try looking in your local community to see what non-profits exist and inquire if your services can be of any assistance. Or, take your goodwill one step further and begin your own organization to serve a cause that is dear to your heart.

Remember this: you became a consultant because you strongly feel that you can use your talents to help other people. Take that feeling one step further and help those who really need it, but cannot afford to pay you. You will not only be boosting your public image, you will be boosting your spirit.

In Conclusion

In this chapter, we have talked about getting more involved in the consulting community, as well as getting involved in your local community. We have listed a few consulting organizations that you may want to become a member of. And, we have also talked about donating your services to non-profit organizations.

Closing Thoughts

This concludes our discussion on Consulting. Hopefully, you have learned about the Consulting profession and have determined that it's the path for you. Starting a new business is never easy. It takes a lot of hard work and endurance. But when you fully understand the process you are about to undertake, and you plan accordingly, you will be poised for success.

As a consultant, you will be using your talent and expertise to aid others in their endeavors. There cannot be a more rewarding feeling than helping others achieve their goals for success, because you will achieve your own success as a result. Now is the time to take destiny in hand and begin the journey towards self-employment.

Appendices

The following appendices are also available in electronic format at http://www.entrepreneurbootcamp.com.

Appendix 1: Basic Business Startup Checklist

Appendix 2: Sample Consulting Proposal

Appendix 3: Sample Consulting Contrac

Appendix 4: Sample Consulting Invoices

Appendix 5: Marketing Plan Template

Appendix 6: Website References

Appendix 1: Basic Business Startup Checklist

1. Name your business. (Check to make sure the name is available, and then trademark your name).
2. Register domain name for website.
3. Obtain any patents for your product/service.
4. Register any copyrights.
5. Decide where your base of operations for your business will be.
6. Budget your startup costs.
7. Write your business plan.
8. Seek out potential investors and pitch your business plan in order to raise capital.
9. Choose your business entity.
10. Hire an attorney to formally register your business entity.
11. Apply for any required business license or permit.
12. Check with local, state and federal government agencies for any applicable regulations.
13. File for Federal employer identification number (if needed).
14. File for state employer identification number (if needed).
15. Design and launch website (assess the best solution either custom or CMS).
16. Set up business phone lines & high-speed Internet (possibly use a PBX/Phone answering service and Internet faxing).
17. Set up all utilities for your location.
18. Choose a bank and set up business checking account.
19. Obtain proper insurance (liability insurance and the like).
20. Obtain appropriate Worker's Compensation Insurance.
21. Hire accountant and/or purchase accounting software.
22. Design and print business cards, business letterhead & stationery.
23. Fully equip office with needed furniture and office supplies.

24. Line up distributors and product suppliers (if relevant).
25. Search for experts who can serve on your Advisory Board.
26. Develop your Marketing Strategy and begin product promotion.

DOWNLOAD

http://authr.me/cKa

Appendix 2: Sample Consulting Proposal

The following consulting proposal should be customized for your particular consulting business. When used it should be printed on your company letterhead.

Dear [Recipient],

I wanted to thank you for the [phone call / meeting] and for the opportunity to work with [Recipient Company]. As per our conversation, I have identified [services to provide] in regards to [project name]. After considering your concerns, I am providing a proposal that outlines deliverables and will ensure that [effective solution]. This project will result in [explain the desired result].

This proposal includes the following sections:

- Scope of Work
  o Deliverables
- Schedule & Fees
- Authorization
- Scope of Work

[The scope of work should identify key project steps to be performed. You can break each section using a bold heading. Only go into as much detail as you believe the client might need to make a decision.

[Project Item]

[Description]

Deliverables

Identify any deliverables in the form of analysis, documentation, and final working product or environment.

[list out in bullet format each of the specific deliverables required to successfully complete the project.]

Include a short paragraph or sentence that explains that the deliverables can be modified in name, but the overall project deliverable will meet the scope of work objectives. This allows you to provide more flexible solutions and documentation.

Schedule & Fees

[Describe when and where the work will take place and what the nature of the work environment will be. The following is an example of an actual proposal for one of my clients.

[Company Name] agrees to pay consulting fees of [x]/hr ($[x] per day), with an original retainer of [x] hours at ($x,xxx.xx) for work to be completed on or before [Date]. Additional billing will occur in 5-day intervals (after the completion of 5 days of work). Payment terms are 10 days.

Issues of confidentiality, client relationships, and discussion regarding proprietary products, services, or relationships, in addition to documents created as part of this consulting relationship, are the property of [Client Name].

Appropriate access to vendors, customers, contacts, and administrative system access will be provided by [Client Name] as required to complete any assigned projects.

[Client Name] will provide an office space with Internet access, phone, fax, and copier as needed for project work.

Both parties (myself and [Client Name]) will make every effort to ensure timely answers to questions as related to the project engagement.

Authorization

[Client Name] agrees to the scope of work as outlined on the above proposal dated **[Date].** [Consultant or Consulting Organization] is directed to proceed with the scheduling as outlined on the proposal. Authorization and commencement of above work requires a signed copy of this proposal and a work initiation payment of $x,xxx made payable to [Consultant or Consulting Organization]. Change orders for work outside of the scope of this agreement will be submitted to a [Client Name] representative (assumed to be [Primary Contact or Authorized Contact) authorized to approve such work. Final payment for all integration labor shall be due no later than the day of completion/day of delivery.

This proposal is valid for 30 days from the proposal date.

Agreed To:

Date:

Authorized [Client Name] Representative

As we move forward, I can assist in the procurement of all necessary hardware or software and provide the talent/staff necessary for the integration work. In addition, per our discussion, I can assist in the [Client Name] stated objective of reaching a "paperless office" environment.

These projects can be discussed as time permits and additional system information is gathered.

DOWNLOAD

http://authr.me/cKb

Appendix 3: Sample Consulting Contract

This Consulting Agreement (the "Agreement") is entered into this [specify date] by and between [Name of Consultant], an individual, ("Consultant") and [Name of Company] (the "Company").

RECITALS

WHEREAS, the Company is in need of assistance in the [specify] support area; and

WHEREAS, Consultant has agreed to perform consulting work for the Company in providing [specify] support and consulting services and other related activities as directed by the Company;

NOW, THEREFORE, the parties hereby agree as follows:

1. Consultant's Services. Consultant shall be available and shall provide to the Company professional consulting services in the area of [specify] support ("Consulting services") as requested.

2. Consideration.

A. RATE. In consideration for the Consulting Services to be performed by Consultant under this Agreement, the Company will pay Consultant at the rate of [specify rate] per hour for time spent on Consulting Services. Consultant shall submit written, signed reports of the time spent performing Consulting Services, itemizing in reasonable detail the dates on which services were performed, the number of hours spent on such dates and a brief description of the services rendered. The Company shall pay Consultant the amounts due pursuant to submitted reports within 14 days after such reports are received by the Company.

B. EXPENSES. Additionally, the Company will pay Consultant for the following expenses incurred while the Agreement between Consultant and the Company exists:

- All travel expenses to and from all work sites
- Meal expenses;
- Administrative expenses;
- Lodging Expenses if work demands overnight stays; and
- Miscellaneous travel-related expenses (parking and tolls.

Consultant shall submit written documentation and receipts where available itemizing the dates on which expenses were incurred. The Company shall pay Consultant the amounts due pursuant to submitted reports within 14 days after a report is received by the Company.

3. Independent Contractor. Nothing herein shall be construed to create an employer-employee relationship between the Company and Consultant. Consultant is an independent contractor and not an employee of the Company or any of its subsidiaries or affiliates. The consideration set forth in Section 2 shall be the sole consideration due Consultant for the services rendered hereunder. It is understood that the Company will not withhold any amounts for payment of taxes from the compensation of Consultant hereunder. Consultant will not represent to be or hold herself out as an employee of the Company.

4. Confidentiality. In the course of performing Consulting Services, the parties recognize that Consultant may come in contact with or become familiar with information which the Company or its subsidiaries or affiliates may consider confidential. This information may include, but is not limited to, information pertaining to the Company [specify] systems, which information may be of value to a competitor. Consultant agrees to keep all such information confidential and not to discuss or divulge it to anyone other than appropriate Company personnel or their designees.

5. Term. This Agreement shall commence on [specify date] and shall terminate on [specify date], unless earlier terminated by either party hereto. Either party may terminate this Agreement upon Thirty (30) days prior written notice. The Company may, at its option, renew this Agreement for an additional One (1) year term on the same terms and conditions as set forth herein by giving notice to Consultant of such intent to renew on or before [specify date].

6. Notice. Any notice or communication permitted or required by this Agreement shall be deemed effective when personally delivered or deposited, postage prepaid, in the first class mail of the United States properly addressed to the appropriate party at the address set forth below:

1. Notices to Consultant: [specify address]
2. Notices to the Company: [specify address]

7. Miscellaneous.

7.1 Entire Agreement and Amendments. This Agreement constitutes the entire agreement of the parties with regard to the subject matter hereof, and replaces and supersedes all other agreements or understandings, whether written or oral. No amendment or extension of the Agreement shall be binding unless in writing and signed by both parties.

7.2 Binding Effect, Assignment. This Agreement shall be binding upon and shall inure to the benefit of Consultant and the Company and to the Company's successors and assigns. Nothing in this Agreement shall be construed to permit the assignment by Consultant of any of its rights or obligations hereunder, and such assignment is expressly prohibited without the prior written consent of the Company.

7.3 Governing Law, Severability. This Agreement shall be governed by the laws of the State of [specify]. The invalidity or unenforceability of any provision of the Agreement shall not affect the validity or enforceability of any other provision.

WHEREFORE, the parties have executed this Agreement as of the date first written above.

[COMPANY NAME]
By:

_____

[Date]

[CONSULTANT NAME]
By:

_____

[Date]

DOWNLOAD

http://authr.me/cKc

Appendix 4: Sample Consulting Invoices

INVOICE   Invoice # 2470

Generic Company
865 South Main Street
Los Angeles, CA 90026
555-555-5555
info@genericcompany.com
www.genericcompany.com
Federal tax # 999999999

DOWNLOAD

http://authr.me/cKd

February 15, 2010

Attention: Betty Johnson, A/P
Sample Client Inc
1234 Mockingbird Lane
Los Angeles, CA 90026
555-555-555

Description: Business Consulting for Project X

Work Performed	Hours	Rate	Total
Business consulting	4 hours	$120.00	$480.00
TOTAL			**$480.00**

Terms: To be paid within 20 business days of invoice date.
Please make all checks payable to Generic Company.
Unpaid balances will accrue interest at 10% per annum,
calculated monthly.

All work is complete! Thanks for your business.

Appendix 5: Marketing Plan Template

Marketing is all about finding, reaching and selling to clients. Chapter 4 describes in detail the parts of your marketing plan and methods you will use to market your new business.

The following marketing plan template will help you to organize your marketing plan. The template is an excerpt from the SCORE Association Business Plan Template. For more templates and resources visit http://www.entrepreneurbootcamp.com or http://www.score.org.

DOWNLOAD

http://authr.me/cJS

Marketing Plan

Market research - Why?
No matter how good your product and your service, the venture cannot succeed without effective marketing. And this begins with careful, systematic research. It is very dangerous to assume that you already know about your intended market. You need to do market research to make sure you're on track. Use the business planning process as your opportunity to uncover data and to question your marketing efforts. Your time will be well spent.

Market research - How?
There are two kinds of market research: primary and secondary.

Secondary research means using published information such as industry profiles, trade journals, newspapers, magazines, census data, and demographic profiles. This type of information is available in public libraries, industry associations, chambers of commerce, from vendors who sell to your industry, and from government agencies.

Start with your local library. Most librarians are pleased to guide you through their business data collection. You will be amazed at what is there. There are more online sources than you could possibly use. Your chamber of commerce has good information on the local area. Trade associations and trade publications often have excellent industry-specific data.

Primary research means gathering your own data. For example, you could do your own traffic count at a proposed location, use the yellow pages to identify competitors, and do surveys or focus-group interviews to learn about consumer preferences. Professional market research can be very costly, but there are many books that show small business owners how to do effective research themselves.

In your marketing plan, be as specific as possible; give statistics, numbers, and sources. The marketing plan will be the basis, later on, of the all-important sales projection.

Economics

Facts about your industry:

- What is the total size of your market?

- What percent share of the market will you have? (This is important only if you think you will be a major factor in the market.)

- Current demand in target market.

- Trends in target market—growth trends, trends in consumer preferences, and trends in product development.

- Growth potential and opportunity for a business of your size.

- What barriers to entry do you face in entering this market with your new company? Some typical barriers are:

  - High capital costs
  - High production costs
  - High marketing costs
  - Consumer acceptance and brand recognition
  - Training and skills
  - Unique technology and patents
  - Unions
  - Shipping costs
  - Tariff barriers and quotas

- And of course, how will you overcome the barriers?
- How could the following affect your company?
  - Change in technology
  - Change in government regulations
  - Change in the economy
  - Change in your industry

Product

In the *Products and Services* section, you described your products and services as you see them. Now describe them from your customers' point of view.

Features and Benefits

List all of your major products or services.

For each product or service:

- Describe the most important features. What is special about it?
- Describe the benefits. That is, what will the product do for the customer?

Note the difference between features and benefits, and think about them. For example, a house that gives shelter and lasts a long time is made with certain materials and to a certain design; those are its features. Its benefits include pride of ownership, financial security, providing for the family, and inclusion in a neighborhood. You build features into your product so that you can sell the benefits.

What after-sale services will you give? Some examples are delivery, warranty, service contracts, support, follow-up, and refund policy.

Customers
Identify your targeted customers, their characteristics, and their geographic locations, otherwise known as their demographics.

The description will be completely different depending on whether you plan to sell to other businesses or directly to consumers. If you sell a consumer product, but sell it through a channel of distributors, wholesalers, and retailers, you must carefully analyze both the end consumer and the middleman businesses to which you sell.

You may have more than one customer group. Identify the most important groups. Then, for each customer group, construct what is called a demographic profile:

- Age
- Gender
- Location
- Income level

- Social class and occupation
- Education
- Other (specific to your industry)
- Other (specific to your industry)

For business customers, the demographic factors might be:
- Industry (or portion of an industry)
- Location
- Size of firm
- Quality, technology, and price preferences
- Other (specific to your industry)
- Other (specific to your industry)

Competition
What products and companies will compete with you?

List your major competitors:

(Names and addresses)

Will they compete with you across the board, or just for certain products, certain customers, or in certain locations?

Will you have important indirect competitors? (For example, video rental stores compete with theaters, although they are different types of businesses.)

How will your products or services compare with the competition?

Use the following Competitive Analysis table to compare your company with your two most important competitors. In the first column are key competitive factors. Since these vary from one industry to another, you may want to customize the list of factors.

In the column labeled **Me**, state how you honestly think you will stack up in customers' minds. Then check whether you think this factor will be a strength or a weakness for you. Sometimes it is hard to analyze our own weaknesses. Try to be very honest here. Better yet, get some disinterested strangers to assess you. This can be a real eye-opener. And remember that you cannot be all things to all people. In fact, trying to be causes many business failures because efforts become scattered and diluted. You want an honest assessment of your firm's strong and weak points.

Now analyze each major competitor. In a few words, state how you think they compare.

In the final column, estimate the importance of each competitive factor to the customer. 1 = critical; 5 = not very important.

Table 1: Competitive Analysis

Factor	Me	Strength	Weakness	Competitor A	Competitor B	Importance to Customer
Products						
Price						
Quality						
Selection						
Service						
Reliability						
Stability						
Expertise						

Factor	Me	Strength	Weakness	Competitor A	Competitor B	Importance to Customer
Company Reputation						
Location						
Appearance						
Sales Method						
Credit Policies						
Advertising						
Image						

Now, write a short paragraph stating your competitive advantages and disadvantages.

Niche

Now that you have systematically analyzed your industry, your product, your customers, and the competition, you should have a clear picture of where your company fits into the world.

In one short paragraph, define

DOWNLOAD

http://authr.me/cKh

your niche, your unique corner of the market.

Strategy
Now outline a marketing strategy that is consistent with
your niche.

Promotion

How will you get the word out to customers?

Advertising: What media, why, and how often? Why this
mix and not some other?

Have you identified low-cost methods to get the most out of
your promotional budget?

Will you use methods other than paid advertising, such as
trade shows, catalogs, dealer incentives, word of mouth
(how will you stimulate it?), and network of friends or
professionals?

What image do you want to project? How do you want
customers to see you?

In addition to advertising, what plans do you have for
graphic image support? This includes things like logo
design, cards and letterhead, brochures, signage, and
interior design (if customers come to your place of
business).

Should you have a system to identify repeat customers and
then systematically contact them?

Promotional Budget

How much will you spend on the items listed above?

Before startup? (These numbers will go into your startup
budget.)

Ongoing? (These numbers will go into your operating plan
budget.)

Pricing

Explain your method or methods of setting prices. For most small businesses, having the lowest price is not a good policy. It robs you of needed profit margin; customers may not care as much about price as you think; and large competitors can underprice you anyway. Usually you will do better to have average prices and compete on quality and service.

Does your pricing strategy fit with what was revealed in your competitive analysis?

Compare your prices with those of the competition. Are they higher, lower, the same? Why?

How important is price as a competitive factor? Do your intended customers really make their purchase decisions mostly on price?

What will be your customer service and credit policies?

Proposed Location

Probably you do not have a precise location picked out yet. This is the time to think about what you want and need in a location. Many startups run successfully from home for a while.

You will describe your physical needs later, in the *Operational Plan* section. Here, analyze your location criteria as they will affect your customers.

Is your location important to your customers? If yes, how?

If customers come to your place of business:

Is it convenient? Parking? Interior spaces? Not out of the way?

Is it consistent with your image?

Is it what customers want and expect?

Where is the competition located? Is it better for you to be near them (like car dealers or fast food restaurants) or distant (like convenience food stores)?

Distribution Channels

How do you sell your products or services?

Retail

Direct (mail order, Web, catalog)

Wholesale

Your own sales force

Agents

Independent representatives

Bid on contracts

Sales Forecast
Now that you have described your products, services, customers, markets, and marketing plans in detail, it's time to attach some numbers to your plan. Use a sales forecast spreadsheet to prepare a month-by-month projection. The forecast should be based on your historical sales, the marketing strategies that you have just described your market research, and industry data, if available.

You may want to do two forecasts: 1) a "best guess", which is what you really expect, and 2) a "worst case" low estimate that you are confident you can reach no matter what happens.

Remember to keep notes on your research and your assumptions as you build this sales forecast and all subsequent spreadsheets in the plan. This is critical if you are going to present it to funding sources.

Appendix 6: Website References

Website	URL	Details
Association of Image Consultants International	www.aici.org	AICI place for Image consultants to become certified, network with other image consultants and gain visibility by being a listed member on their website.
Association of Professional Consultants	www.consultapc.org	The APC is a referral organization that allows visitors to search a list of qualified and certified consultants from all manner of industries. For consultants, they can be listed in the online directly, and also network with other members.
BNI	www.bni.com	BNI is an online business networking organization. Members can share ideas, contacts as well as business referrals.
Business.com	www.business.com	Business.com is a Business Search Engine and

Website	URL	Details
		directory. It's a place where business owners can search for services and providers
Crowd Spring	www.crowdspring.com	CrowdSpring is another virtual marketplace where employers can find the creative talent they need to help with their logo design. The site is geared towards graphic and logo designers, as well as some creative writers.
Facebook	www.facebook.com	Facebook is a social networking website where members create an online community of "friends". Businesses can create fan pages and keep in contact with consumers.
Freelancer	www.freelancer.com	Freelancer is a global freelance project bidding website that assists

14

Website	URL	Details
		freelancers from all manner of industries find employers looking to hire temporary and project based work. The site allows employers to post jobs and freelancers to bid on those jobs, and then be hired and paid through the website.
Go Daddy	www.GoDaddy.com	Go Daddy is a website hosting service that allows users to search and register available website names and urls, and build a website from different templates for a variety of monthly prices.
Human Resources Consultants Association	www.hrca.com	HRCA is a professional association for Human Resources consultants, whether individuals or consulting firms.

Website	URL	Details
		They offer a searchable database of qualified HR consultants to help start-ups with staffing strategies.
Independent Computer Consultant Association	www.icaa.org	ICAA is an online consulting organization for computer consultants. Members can network and also offer information and support to businesses.
Institute of Management Consultants	www.imcusa.org	The IMC is an online consulting organization for image consultants to network and benefit from personal referrals as well as being listed on an online searchable directory.
Internal Revenue Service	www.irs.gov	The IRS website gives facts, information and a list of resources for individuals and

Website	URL	Details
		businesses needing to tax information. IRS forms available for download.
iUtility	www.iUtility.com	Internet domain registration website where you can search and register available website names, create a website, and advertise your website on a WHOIS listing directly for different monthly prices.
LeTip	www.letip.com	LeTip is a professional business leads organization. Members can gain business through personal referrals.
LinkedIn	www.linkedin.com	LinkedIn is a business professional social networking website. Members create profiles and can post interactive resumes as well as join groups of related professionals.

Website	URL	Details
Market Research	www.marketresearch.com	Market Research is an online assemblage of market research information with over 250,000 reports from over 600 providers covering almost all markets and providers. Members can browse the available reports and order the ones you want. \
oDesk	www.oDesk.com	ODesk is a virtual office where employers can look for virtual workers who they can hire on an hourly basis and monitor the work they are doing through the website.
Professional and Technical Consulting Association	www.patca.org	PATCA is a consulting referral organization that covers a wide

Website	URL	Details
		variety of specializations. It is a non-profit organization that is run by consultants that offers networking opportunities for its members, as well as a free referral service.
Qualitative Research Consultants Association	www.qrca.org	QRCA is a listing of consultants that offer information for businesses looking to obtain market research and consumer habit information through surveys, focus groups, and other research methods.
vWorker (formerly RentACoder)	www.vworker.com	vWorker is a virtual marketplace where businesses can post jobs, accept bids, and then hire virtual computer programmers on either a project or short-term basis.

Website	URL	Details
Score	www.score.org	SCORE is a non-profit organization that offers free and confidential advice to entrepreneurs and small businesses.
Small Business Administration	www.sba.gov	The SBA website offers programs and services to aid new small businesses obtain the reference materials they need as well as many business planning tools and local resources.
Entrepreneur Boot Camp Books	www.entrepreneurbootcamp.com	Entrepreneur Boot Camp Books offers a series of books on how to start a new business. The site lists many different reference websites and links you'll need in order to form a business, as well as useful checklists and forms.
Tech Serve Alliance	www.techservealliance.org	TSA is an association of IT businesses, consultants and providers that

Website	URL	Details
		provides a collaborative networking and information sharing service for members.
Twitter	www.twitter.com	Twitter is a truncated blogging service where members can "tweet" information up to 140 characters. Followers of a tweet will get notification to their Twitter account, email and cell phones as a text message.
US Copyright Office	www.copyright.gov	The Copyright Office website will allow you to register your copyright material and pay the required fees, either through the website or by downloading the appropriate forms. They also serve as a resource for information about copyrights.
US Patent & Trade Office	www.uspto.gov	The USPTO website offers

Website	URL	Details
		information on obtaining and maintaining patents as well as business trademarks. You can also download the required application forms to file for a patent or trademark.
VeriSign	www.verisign.com	VeriSign offers online identity and authentication services, as well as privacy controls for websites accepting payments over the internet. They aid in financial transactions and help keep shared information private.
Vertical Answer	www.verticalanswer .com	Remotely hosted virtual PBX and toll free number service provider.
YouTube	www.youtube.com	YouTube is a video posting and sharing website where anyone can upload a short video that can be browsed by any visitor to the site.

Glossary of Terms

Accredited Investor	Used by the SEC in Regulation D for establishing those investors that are permitted to invest in certain high risk investments; based on net worth, generally wealthy organizations or individuals.
Advertising	A specific action taken to promote a product or service.
Advisory board	A board of qualified professionals who serve to offer expertise and advice on various business strategies and operations.
Angel investor	A wealthy individual that chooses to invest in new and emerging businesses.
Balance sheet	A snapshot look at the assets, liabilities and equity in a business.
Barriers to entry	Any obstacle that is present in an industry which can restrict the entry of new products, including lack of access to materials and distribution channels, or the lack of

property or technology which in turn increases risk.

Blog

An online log of thoughts, either personal or business in nature.

Branding

Developing a clear identity for a business and/or specific product or service.

Break-even point

The point a business reaches when they will not make money nor lose money on a certain product or service.

Brochure

A folded or bound document that presents the attributes and services a business provides, used for marketing purposes.

Budget

The careful planning of business operations based on the projections of income and expenses over any number of periods.

Business assets

Assets of a business which can be tangible (physical) and intangible (theoretical).

Business description segment	A section of a business plan that will describe the proposed business, describe the product or service to be sold, explain why the business will be profitable, and list goals for future growth.
Business environment	The environment surrounding a business – including the opportunities and risks inherent in selling a product or service.
Business plan	A written document which explains in detail all the facets of a proposed new business. Must include what the new business is, what is being sold, how much money is needed and what profits are expected.
Business valuation	Calculating the value of a business by a variety of methods and formulas.
Buyer	The business or individual who directly pays the consultant for their services.

Calculated risk taking	When entrepreneurs study all expected risks, and think of solutions that will help them combat those risks, thus making the potential risks less threatening.
Capital	The net worth of a business; that is, the amount by which its assets exceed its liabilities.
Capital budgeting	A budgeting method which determines cash flow from investments and ways to increase profitability from investments.
Career risk	The risk an entrepreneur takes in leaving a current job to start a new business which has a possibility of failure.
Cash-flow budget	Forecasts all cash inflows and cash outflows to determine a company's cash on hand at any given time.
Cash-flow statement	Gives a clear picture of how much cash comes into a business and how much cash flows out of a business.
Client	Either a business or an individual that engages a

consultant to perform a service to achieve desired results.

Close corporation	A corporation in which stock is only held by a few individuals and is not for sale to the general public.
Code of conduct	The guidelines and ethical practices which a business must stick to.
Collection Agency	A third party that will pursue payment of an unpaid balance for a portion of the balance due.
Collective entrepreneurship	The combined skills of a group of individuals who come together to create and innovate.
Common stock	Securities representing equity ownership in a corporation, providing voting rights, and entitling the holder to a share of the company's success through dividends and/or capital appreciation.
Community demographics	The makeup of consumers within a select community.

Competitive analysis	Examination of the practices of all competitors within a business' industry.
Consultant	A person who possesses a certain talent, skill or expertise that when applied can improve the situation of another individual or business.
Consulting contract	An official agreement between the consultant and the buyer to perform a specified service in return for monetary compensation.
Consulting proposal	A written summation of the service a consultant is offering.
Consumer pricing	Evaluating the perceived value of a product or service by the consumer to set a competitive price.
Consumer driven philosophy	Marketing research where the emphasis is placed on the wants and needs of the targeted consumer.

Continuous improvement	Increasing the quality of a product or service slowly and steadily over time.
Copyright	Legal protection over everything written including books, catalogues, lists, manuals, advertisements, photographs, websites, film, video & audio works, architectural designs, computer software and hardware.
Corporate entrepreneurship	A company which seeks to foster entrepreneurial thinking and innovation by employees within the company. Also referred to as Intrapreneurship.
Corporation	A legal business structure which is a separate entity from the owners and is overseen by federal and state regulations. A corporation is begun when shareholders transfer money into the business in return for stock.

Creative process

A process of development including the gaining of knowledge, the formation of an idea, and the development of that idea into a physical product or service.

Creativity

New ideas which result in the creation of a new process, or improvement of a current process.

Critical risks segment

A section within a business plan which talks about the potential risks and obstacles a new business might take, as well as steps that will be taken to combat those risks.

Culture

Shared values and beliefs among those within a business.

Customer availability

Gaining potential consumers before the business is launched.

Daily activity log

A time keeping method for consultants to keep track of time spent on business activities relating to a project.

Data collection sheets

Informational sheets used to gather data pertaining to performance so problems can be analyzed.

Debt financing	When a business borrows money for operations or new purchases can be either long-term or short-term.
Delegating	Giving tasks over to other trained employees so as to save time.
Design patent	Owner is granted exclusive rights over the production, process and subsequent sale of a product or service. (Term is usually 14 years).
Direct foreign investment	Foreign operations which are controlled domestically.
Diversified marketing	A marketing strategy which examines the life cycle of individual products and services and seeks out different approaches for each one.
Domain name	The name of a business which is included in a web address, or URL, followed by a domain organization such as .com or

.net.

Domestic corporation	A corporation which does business in the United States.
Domestic international sales corporation (DISC)	A legal business entity that has tax benefits for businesses that export outside the United States.
Drive to achieve	The desire within an individual to excel against any odds and to reach designated goals.
E-commerce	The marketing, promotion, buying and selling of goods and services electronically over the internet.
Economic base	The type of employment and subsequent income of consumers in a given area.
Ecovision	A leadership style which stresses flexibility in business operations due to the changing economic and social environment.
Emotional bias	When one believes the business is worth more than

others believe it is worth.

Employee stock ownership plan (ESOP)	Passing along eventual control of the corporation to the employees in lieu of designating a successor.
Empowerment	Believing one has the power to take control and make decisions.
Entrepreneur	An individual who is an innovator; takes steps to create a new idea; turn the idea into a viable product or service; then creates a new business to introduce that product or service to the marketplace.
Entrepreneurial assessment	Making an assessment in regards to the entrepreneur, the new business and the surrounding environment.
Entrepreneurial behavior	The decision to take control and start a new business.
Entrepreneurial culture	A business culture which is typically informal, with a focus on creativity and the pursuit of

new opportunities.

Entrepreneurial leadership	The ability of an entrepreneur to think strategically and creatively in order to implement changes within an organization.
Entrepreneurial leveraged buyout (ELBO)	A sale where at least two-thirds of the purchase is from financing.
Entrepreneurial management	Applying an entrepreneurial spirit in the management of a business.
Entrepreneurial marketing	Attempting to develop a specific niche within an industry with a new innovation.
Entrepreneurial motivation	The drive of an entrepreneur to maintain an entrepreneurial spirit in all their actions.
Entrepreneurial perspective	Characteristics of an entrepreneur which are fostered in an individual and therefore shapes their way of thinking.

Entrepreneurship	The process of creating a new business, then assuming the risks of a new business.
Environmental assessment	Evaluating the current economic environment and the current governmental regulations affecting that environment.
Environmental awareness	An awareness and subsequent desire to preserve natural resources and the environment.
Equity financing	The offering of ownership in a business in return for investment capital.
Ethics	Principles that outline a behavior and govern over right and wrong actions.
Expenses	Any cost the business is obligated to pay out. Can be grouped in a number of ways, including those that are fixed (like rent) and those that are variable (like utilities).
Experimentation	The trial and error done when researching new products and

processes.

Exporting	Selling a product internationally.
External optimism	The optimism present in entrepreneurs that is a driving factor for success.
External problems	Any problem or obstacle that arises from consumers, the market, competition and the external expansion of the business.
External resources	Resources obtained from outside the business.
Feasibility criteria approach	Factors which will help an entrepreneur determine the viability of their new business.
Fee	A monetary payment made to a consultant in return for services.
Finance company	A lender which will lend money to a business against the assets of a business (such as inventory).

Financial risk	The cash and business resources which are at risk in the event of failure.
Financial segment	The portion of the business plan which will present financial forecasts and budgets for the new business.
Five minute reading	The process a potential investor will use when quickly reviewing a business plan.
Fixed cost	A cost that does not depend upon business activity such as rent or salaries.
Foreign corporation	A corporation which does business outside of the United States.
Foreign economic trends	Evaluating the current business market in foreign countries; taking into account such factors as the gross national product, unemployment rates, and consumer price indexes.
Franchise	An agreement by which a business owner allows another to sell trademarked products

and services for a fee.

Freelance	To outsource talent or expertise to an employer on a short-term or project-by-project basis.
Funding gap	A barrier faced by women entrepreneurs when they attempt to find financing for a new business.
General partner	A partner in a partnership who has unlimited liability and management over a company's operations.
Growth of sales	The predicted growth pattern for the sales of a new product or service.
Harvest strategy	A decision to exit a business, whether through a sale or public offering.
High growth venture	When the predicted sales are high enough to attract interest from potential investors.
Immersion in business	When an entrepreneur places their entire focus into the new

business and does not leave any time for personal activities.

Importing	Buying and distributing foreign goods within the Unites States.
Income statement	Forecasts sales minus cost of goods sold and general & administrative expenses; will show both current numbers and projected numbers. Also called a Profit & Loss Statement.
Incremental innovation	The slow introduction of a new innovation into new markets.
Initial public offering (IPO)	The opening up of stock in a company for sale to the general public on the stock exchange.
Innovation	Taking an opportunity and thinking of a creative idea in which to capitalize on the opportunity.
Intellectual property right	The protection of rights in the form of patents, trademarks, copyrights and trade secrets

against use by others.

Internet marketing — Marketing and promoting a business over the internet whether through a business website, email, or through various social networking sites.

Internet — An interconnected network accessible through a computer; a global distribution channel for goods, services and human resources.

Intracapital — Capital which is set aside by the entrepreneur for future research & development.

Intrapreneurship — An action taken by a large company or corporation to foster innovation and the entrepreneurial spirit within the business to foster new growth.

Invention — An innovation that creates a new product/service/process that is entirely new and untried before.

Joint venture	When more than one company bands together to own an organization, usually for doing business in foreign markets.
Lead	Receiving the name and contact information for a potential customer from any resource.
Leveraged buyout (LBO)	The acquisition of another company using a large amount of borrowed funds using the assets of the acquired company as collateral.
Licensing	Permission granted by a business to another business or individual allowing them to manufacture and/or sell a product or service which is trademarked, in return for a fee.
Lifecycle stages	The different parts of the natural life cycle of a business including birth, development, growth, stabilization, expansion or decline.
Lifestyle venture	A business venture in which the entrepreneur creates out of a desire for independence, financial freedom and

complete control.

Limited liability	A limit placed on the liability responsibility of a limited partner or shareholder.
Limited liability company (LLC)	A relatively new business entity that has the liability protection of a corporation and the tax benefits of a partnership.
Limited liability partnership (LLP)	A form of partnership where all partners are limited partners and have restricted personal liability and greater tax advantages than a normal partnership.
Limited partnership	A partnership that allows for one or more general partners who have unlimited liability and complete control over the business; and the remaining are limited partners who have limited liability and no business control.
Liquidation	To pay off a debt by selling a company's assets.

Logo

A graphic design or image that gives a visual to a business and business name.

Macro view of entrepreneurship

Looking at a wide variety of factors that can determine the success or failure of a new entrepreneurial start-up.

Management

The organization and coordination of business activities and individuals to achieve a set of goals.

Management segment

A part of a business plan that details more about the owner, the management team, the type of business and any advisors or board of directors.

Manufacturing segment

The part of a business plan which discusses the business location and the needs of starting up production: inventory needs, production needs, suppliers and labor needs.

Market

A group of consumers (current or potential) who have needs for a specific type of product or service.

Market niche	A smaller group within a larger market with very specific needs in common.
Market planning	A set of different methods and channels with which to get the knowledge of a product or service to a consumer.
Market segmentation	Identifying certain characteristics that set a group of consumers apart from other consumers.
Market value	A business valuation method which seeks to determine the value of a business based on prices paid for similar businesses.
Marketability	Analyzing a business to determine if the business will have success in the market.
Marketing	The strategy to find customers and then promote your product or service to entice customers to buy your product or service.

Marketing research	Compiling all relevant consumer and market data then analyzing the information.
Marketing segment	A part of a business plan that describes the market and the strategy of the business to enter the market and promote directly to the consumer.
Measures of success	The accomplishments of small tasks and goals in regards to a project that shows the project is on track to meeting its overall objective.
Milestones	Small easily attainable goals along the timeline of a business' greater goal.
Minority-owned business	A business owned by a minority group, including African Americans, Hispanics, and Asians among others.
Mixed costs	A mixture of both fixed and variable costs.
Multidimensional approach	Looking at all facets of entrepreneurship from the entrepreneur, to the business, the startup process and the

	surrounding environment.
National Federation of Independent Business (NFIB)	A business advocacy group which represents small businesses in D.C. and all 50 state capitals, boasting over 600,000 business owners.
Nepotism	Preferring relatives over other non-related candidates when filling employment positions.
Networking	Making connections with other business professionals to build a network of contacts.
New products	A product that is currently unknown or not introduced to the public.
Niche	A small group of individuals with very similar characteristics or similar needs for a product or service.
Non-profit corporation	A corporation that does not have an objective of profit; usually a religious, charitable or educational organization.
Objectives	Expected outcomes that when reached, signals that the task

or project was a success.

One sheet	A one-page written document that will list the attributes, past experience, accomplishments and references for a consultant.
Ongoing operations	The day-to-day operations and the ability of the entrepreneur to make decisions that will enhance the productivity of continuing operations.
Online Affiliate Program	Allows third parties to act as independent salespeople for your product or service.
Operating budget	The monthly and annual cost of keeping your business running, including overhead costs (such as rent, utilities, and salaries), any dues and fees, and ongoing marketing and promotions.
Opportunistic marketing	A business which attempts to increase sales by obtaining a larger share of the market.
Opportunity orientation	Entrepreneurs who first and foremost focus on opportunity for growth rather than the business and its resources.

Options	Alternate plans of action or alternate products that a buyer can consider.
Outsourcing	Contracting out of specified services to an outside provider.
Overhead costs	Costs pertaining to operating a business that is not a cost directly associated to a product or service, such as rent or mortgage, and utilities.
Partnership	When two or more business professionals band together to co-own a business.
Patent	A right given by a governmental body to an inventor or entrepreneur giving the exclusive right to produce and sell a new invention (whether method, product or service) for a certain amount of time.
Patent and trademark office	Office within the federal government where all applications for patents and trademarks are filed and granted.

Payback method	A valuation technique under capital budgeting to ascertain the amount of time it will take until the cost of an investment is paid back by new revenue.
Penetration	Measures the degree by which a product or service has effectively reached consumers in a market.
Planning	Spelling out steps of action to achieve a pre-determined goal.
Podcast	The uploading of multimedia files (audio or visual) for playback over a computer or mobile device.
Policies	Policies are principles, rules, and guidelines formulated or adopted by an organization to reach its long-term goals. They are designed to influence and determine all major decisions and actions, and all activities take place within the boundaries set by them.

Preferred stock	A preferential position given to investors in regards to their stock in case the business is dissolved.
Press kit	A group of documents, images and even videos about a business for purposes of promotion. A press kit is usually organized into a folder.
Previous work experience	The past business history of an entrepreneur.
Private corporation	A corporation where only selected investors can hold stock; stock not open to the general public for purchase.
Private debt	Obtaining a financial contribution from an individual that you will treat as a personal loan and pay back with interest.
Private offering	A corporation which will raise capital by offering investment and shares of stock to known business associates and/or family and friends.
Private placement	Securities which are sold by a corporation to raise capital without a public offering of

stock.

Pro Bono	Doing work for an organization or a donating your services to a cause without getting paid.
Pro forma financial statement	A general financial statement that attempts to project the profitability of the business in the future.
Pro forma statements	Projection of a business' financials over a period of time in the future (income statements and balance sheets).
Probability thinking	Seeking out the likelihood of all results when looking to make a decision.
Procedures	Procedures are the specific methods employed to express policies in action in day-to-day operations of the organization. Together, policies and procedures ensure that a point of view held by the governing body of an organization is translated into steps that result in an outcome compatible with that view.

Product availability	How much of a product is available for purchase at any given time.
Product driven philosophy	A focus on the quality of the product to be sold as a marketing strategy and letting the quality of the product sell itself.
Professional corporation	A corporation for certain groups of professionals such as lawyers and accountants.
Profits, sales, and operating ratios	Variables used to determine a company's earning power and value.
Promotion	The overall act of communicating with the public to influence them to buy your product or service.
Public corporation	A government owned corporation formed for a political purpose.
Public offerings	The initial sale of the stock of a company to the general public on the stock exchange.

Radical innovation

A fundamental breakthrough after idea experimentation that must be improved upon and developed.

Reach

The depth and breadth of the business in connecting with consumers.

Reference

A contact who serves to offer a recommendation of an individual to another individual or business.

Reimbursable expense

A business expense that you incur directly due to a project or task that can be recouped from the customer.

Relationship

A continuous interaction based on mutual respect between two business professionals, or between the seller and buyer.

Reliance

The need present in a market for the new product/service and the business' promise to deliver on that need.

Remote worker	An individual that regularly works away from the main office or location where a business normally holds its operations. Also called a **virtual employee**.
Reorganization	A part of bankruptcy where the debtor creates a plan to pay back a portion of debts owed according to a schedule while continuing to stay in business.
Replacement value	A business valuation method which determines the cost it would take to replace a business' assets at current prices.
Research, design, and development segment	Portion of a business plan in which the entrepreneur relays the research and design plan for the new product/service and the processes needed for development.
Responsive marketing	The attention to consumer response in the marketing strategy to attempt to reach a high consumer satisfaction rate.
Retainer	An upfront fee paid to a professional before services begin or on a monthly basis to

be available for services.

Return on investment	A formula used for investor returns by dividing net profit by the initial investment.
Richness	The amount of detail a business can give the consumer about a product/service and the amount of information the business can learn about the consumer in return.
Risk	The threatening uncertainty of an outcome or event.
S corporation	A corporation named for Subchapter S of the IRS Code that allows for increased tax benefits but under more restrictions.
Sales forecast	Predicting future sales by analyzing past sales.
Sales driven philosophy	A marketing strategy that uses a more personal approach to entice consumers to buy the company's product or service.

Scope creep

A project management term that applies to the act of an employer making additional requests and/or increasing the size of a project without warning.

Self-management concept

Personally identifying the management techniques that are required for an entrepreneur to be able to manage a business.

Self publishing

Writing and distributing your own material without obtaining a publisher.

Skimming

Pricing a product or service high to be able to gain short-term profits.

Slogan

A statement that captures what a product or service is selling usually in one sentence.

Small Business Administration

The governmental agency designed to aid small businesses with financial and managerial assistance.

Social media

Encompasses a wide variety of Internet communication

methods between people, including blogs, instant messaging, videos and social networking.

Social obligation	Obedience to social norms.
Social responsibility	A sense of obligation to uphold the values of a society.
Social responsiveness	Being involved in many activities that work to do the most good for society.
Societal environment	The wants, needs and values a society holds and how that affects the operations of a business.
Sole proprietorship	A legal entity which is owned by one person and has no separate identity outside the single owner.
Specialty goods	A good that a consumer places importance on and will go out of their way to locate and purchase.

Specification	The description provided in a patent application along with photographs and diagrams.
Startup activities	A stage in the life cycle of a business when a business is in the process of forming and beginning operations.
Startup budget	The cost to begin a new business including the fees and costs associated with renting an office, setting up utilities, opening a bank account, creating a website, purchasing equipment and supplies, and printing marketing and promotion materials.
Startup problems	Obstacles faced by a beginning business usually due to lack of financing or difficulty in procuring financing.
Staying power	When a business is perceived to have a long life with strong sales.
Stereotyping	Erroneous, relatively fixed, simplistic, and mostly negative generalization (based commonly on bigotry, ignorance, and prejudice) held to be true about certain

individuals or groups.

Stickiness

The features, functions or gimmicks employed by a website that will cause people to want to stay on your site for longer than expected.

Strategy

A plan of action created to achieve a goal.

Strategic alliance

A business relationship between two or more entities for mutual gain.

Strategic planning

Planning future goals for a business and listing the steps that need to be taken to achieve those goals.

Strategic positioning

The attempt to gain a better share of the market and/or draw new consumers into the market.

Technical feasibility

A product or service that has the capability to satisfy the needs and expectations of a consumer.

Telemarketing   Using the telephone to contact
                             a consumer and attempt to sell
                             a product or service.

Temporary worker   An employee brought in on a
                             short-term basis for a specified
                             period of time or for a specified
                             project. When the project or
                             time period ends, so does the
                             employment. Also called a
                             **temp, freelancer, contractual
                             employee** or **seasonal
                             employee**.

Testimonial   An endorsement for your
                             business, usually written, from
                             a satisfied consumer.

Top management   When high level managers in a
support   corporation seek to help out
                             lower-level employees develop
                             entrepreneurial behavior.

Total quality   A managerial style that
management (TQM)   focuses on people and the
                             increase of a company's focus
                             on customer service.

Trade secrets   A type of intellectual property
                             that deals with anything a
                             business considers a secret as
                             to the way they operate,

including plans, product processes, consumer lists, marketing strategies, etc.

Trademark	The name, symbol, slogan or motto that is used by a business and is highly identifiable with that business; able to be protected as a right of use.
Uniqueness	Any business aspect that is considered special or original, also a product or service that attracts consumers by being distinct.
Unlimited liability	When a sole proprietor or general partner takes on complete responsibility for all of the business' actions and debts.
Unsought goods	A good that a consumer does not currently need or actively seek out.
Value	Extent to which a good or service is perceived by its customer to meet his or her

needs or wants, measured by customer's willingness to pay for it. It commonly depends more on the customer's perception of the worth of the product than on its intrinsic value.

Values	Fundamental beliefs that drive human behavior.
Variable cost	A cost that can change depending on business activity such as inventory.
Venture capitalist	An individual who seeks to invest their own money in new business start-ups.
Venture team	A group of individuals who work together to create and develop a new idea.
Viral marketing	Using online word of mouth to spread a message or advertisement, such as having an email forwarded multiple times to people who were not the original

recipient.

Virtual employee	An individual who regularly works away from the main office or location where a business normally holds its operations. Work and communication is done over the internet.
Women entrepreneurs	Women who start and own their own business.

Index

About the Author

Erik Bowman

Erik has been called the father of the online social networking service by creating iMessenger in 1999 and in 2002, he launched the first film industry "crowd funding" service with Film Venture. In 2012, he applied this expertise to create Authr.com; the first crowd funding service dedicated to the book publishing industry.

As an author, speaker, serial entrepreneur and business advisor, Erik has been empowering business owners, start-ups and entrepreneurs to successfully meet their goals for over 20 years. Known for his proactive and innovative approaches to growth, Erik provides branding and marketing initiatives, customized technology solutions, publishing services, and sales strategy for his clients.

LEARN MORE

http://authr.me/cKe

Helping authors, entrepreneurs and business owners, Erik's highly-influential expertise motivates individuals by concentrating on simple, understandable and actionable components to marketing, promoting or enhancing a product or service.

Erik is the author of six books including his best-selling book on Ultimate Marketing Secrets: Social Media Marketing, How to Get Paid to Write Your Book, Your Guaranteed Bestseller: The secrets to making your book a best seller on a budget, and Start It Up! How-To Guides For Business Startups Series of books.

He is also founder and current president of Guanzi Institute® through which he created the Certified Entrepreneur® training program; empowering first-time entrepreneurs, existing business owners and corporate managers with the skills they need to succeed in any industry.

Erik holds a double major in Political Science (summa cum laude) and Philosophy and a master's degree in Education from California State University.

Guanzi Institute®, Certified Entrepreneur® and Entrepreneur Boot Camp® are US Registered Trademarks owned by Erik N Bowman.

More information can be found about Erik N Bowman at http://www.ErikBowman.com

www.ingramcontent.com/pod-product-compliance
Lightning Source LLC
Chambersburg PA
CBHW060526210326
41519CB00014B/3142